I Quit:
Stop Smoking Easily Through the Power of Hypnosis

By

Jess Marion
Sarah Carson
Shawn Carson

Changing Mind Publishing
New York, NY

I Quit: Stop Smoking Through the Power of Hypnosis
Copyright Jess Marion, Sarah Carson, Shawn Carson
© 2014 All rights reserved

Cover Photo- © Ashumskiy | Dreamstime.com - Man\'s Fist Crushing Cigarettes Photo

No part of this book may be reproduced in any manner whatsoever without written permission except in the case of brief quotations embedded in critical articles and reviews. For further information please contact **Changing Mind Publishing** at 545 8th Avenue, Suite 930, New York, NY, 10001.

Table of Contents

Chapter 1:
Deciding Whether It's Time for You to Quit   6

Chapter 2:
The Cigarette Religion   17

Chapter 3:
Let's Get Real   27

Chapter 4:
Tracking Your Habit   31

Chapter 5:
Trading Triggers   35

Chapter 6:
Breaking Through Cravings   42

Chapter 7:
The Backward Spin   48

Chapter 8:
Emotional Freedom Technique   53

Chapter 9:
A Stranger in Your Midst   60

Chapter 10:
Case Study 1   64

Chapter 11:
Case Study 2   75

Chapter 12:
Escaping From Tigers   85

Chapter 13:
6 Steps to Freedom   90

Chapter 14:
Changing Your Life   103

Disclaimer

We are not medically qualified and this book is not intended to be, or replace, medical treatment for diagnosed medical or mental health conditions. If you have such a diagnosis you should consult your physician or mental health professional before using this guide.

If you believe you have a medical or mental health condition you should consult your physician or mental health professional.

Under no circumstances should you cease any form of medical treatment or stop taking any medication, which has been prescribed to you, without seeking medical advice.

If any of the techniques or exercises in this book cause you any kind of mental or emotional distress you should stop immediately and seek appropriate professional help.

While the techniques presented in this book are the result of our successful work with clients and are very powerful we make no guarantees of success. It is the reader's responsibility to change.

Chapter 1: Deciding Whether *It's Time for You to QUIT*

Welcome to the first step of reclaiming your freedom. Now that you have chosen to take this next step, we – Jess, Shawn, and Sarah – will be your guides on this adventure towards your own freedom. In order to make things easy to read going forward we'll just say "I" even when we mean "we".

I would like to start by saying I am not a smoker. I have never been a smoker even though I used to smoke cigarettes. The good news is *you are not a smoker* either. It's true! The first step of creating this change in your life is to realize that *smoking is not who you are*. You were not born a smoker and *you are not a smoker now*. Smoking is simply a behavior, a habit that in the past you made a choice to engage in and a habit *you can decide to drop right now*. Smoking is not a part of your identity.

Now, simply by reading this book, you are making a very different decision. You are deciding to *become a non-smoker*.

You may be wondering if they're not smokers themselves, how can *they guide me* through the process of becoming *a non-smoker. It's easy.* In my career as a hypnotist and coach, I have helped countless people *kick the habit*. This means that I know how to help you navigate your way through the process so that you can *enjoy becoming a non-smoker*. In the course of helping people quit smoking, I've discovered the recurrent patterns that people run in their mind to rationalize maintaining that nasty habit.

Oops, I said it: *nasty habit*. Very often, one of the things that keeps people smoking is that the smoker comes to see a cigarette as an old friend, a companion who has been with them for years, through thick and thin, bad times and good. A cigarette is the friend who wakes them in the morning, helps them deal with the stresses of the day, and enjoy the relaxation of the evening.

But how would you feel about a friend who makes you a nice drink then slips poison into it while you were not looking? Or how would you feel about a friend who steals some bills from the wallet you absent-mindedly laid on the table?

Let's take a brief journey back to World War II, when the smoking epidemic in the US really took hold. Maybe you have a family member who served in that conflict against enemies who threatened our life and liberty. I'm sure you admire the veterans who did such heroic work. And yet one of the rewards our brave servicemen and women received was a regular ration of cigarettes. In fact, cigarette smoking almost doubled during the war years. Consequently, over the years, it is estimated that cigarette companies killed ten times as many veterans of World War II as the Germans and Japanese combined!

So excuse me if I state clearly and for the record, no matter how you feel about cigarettes right now, *cigarettes are not your friend.* No matter how much you may feel now that you rely on cigarettes, *cigarettes are your enemy.* They have already stolen your liberty, and their next target is your life!

In the beginning of my career I used to dread it when clients would call to book a smoking cessation session. You see, in those days I had not yet begun the critical practice of preparing my clients for success. Specifically, I had not yet begun to call them the day before their visit and say something like the following: *"Smoke your last cigarette right now. If you can go one day without smoking, your body has already started to heal. Your blood pressure and pulse will have returned to normal, your blood levels of oxygen will have increased while poisonous carbon monoxide levels will have fallen to normal, and the levels of nicotine in your bloodstream will have decreased by nearly 95%. If you can last one day without smoking, then you have already broken the habit!"*

But in my early days, I hadn't told them to *stop smoking now*, before they even came to their first appointment. Therefore, I knew they would come into my office with their clothes, skin, and hair reeking of stale cigarettes. Speaking to you as someone who detests the stench of stale smoke, I didn't look forward to the fact that I would have to spray air freshener in my small office between that soon-to-be ex-smoker and my next client! This was especially true after a 2-pack-a-day-smoker, racing toward cancer or heart failure; no amount of spraying would get that putrid aroma out of my couch.

The second reason I initially didn't enjoy working with smokers was that I simply didn't know how to work with them. A smoker would come in with their excuses for lighting up, their emotional avoidance of what they knew to be true intellectually, and their years of practicing self-deception. All of which seemed like a tremendous mountain to climb for both the client and me. Nevertheless, I was happily surprised to discover that the more I worked with smokers, the easier it seemed to be for them to quit! The experiences of smoking, the reasons for smoking, and the external triggers for smoking all seemed to fit into bite-size patterns. Soon, whenever a smoker called to ask for an appointment, I could tell in minutes whether they were really *ready to quit*, the likelihood of their being able to do so, and how long it would take for them to actually be *done with that old habit*.

What had initially seemed like a massive mountain was in reality a series of small, easy steps. You just have to *keep taking the next smallest step* and you can *achieve this goal* and enjoy a life of freedom, happiness, and overall wellbeing.

During my own learning process something big shifted inside of me and I discovered the joy of helping people realize that *they could quit easily*. For me this is one of the most rewarding types of work, because when you help *someone to quit smoking, you* help them save their own life. That's right, quitting smoking saves lives; and if you're the smoker, *it might save yours!* Moreover, if you have people who live with you, you are saving more than your own life when you quit smoking.

I don't know your exact reasons for wanting to *let go of cigarettes* but I do know that saving a life, yours, should be high on that list. Take a moment and carefully consider why you really want to quit. Do you want to stop smoking because someone else wants you to, or because *you* want to *do something good for yourself*? If you're reading this book solely because your doctor or your spouse has been on your case, close this book right now. That's right; put it down right now. Only pick it up again when *you're ready to build a healthy future for yourself*. You have to want this change *for yourself*, even though *your family will benefit immensely as well*. If others want you to quit more than you want to, your smoking is their problem and not yours. Making smoking your problem is the first prerequisite.

So why specifically do *you want to stop smoking now?* For some people, it's because of *all of the unpleasant things that cigarettes bring to you*. Perhaps you want to *stop smelling like stale, day-old smoke?* Or is it because you want to *reduce the chance of contracting cancer or heart disease?* Perhaps it's because you want to *stop feeling bad*.

One of the big reasons clients want to quit is because they're already feeling the effects of smoking. They have less energy. It's harder to breathe. And they know they just don't feel like themselves. Another big reason is that they know a friend or family member who died from smoking-related causes, and they definitely don't want to go that route.

Of course, on the flipside, many people think of the benefits that come with being a non-smoker. One of the first things that come to mind is *saving money every day*. Another is *having more energy*. And many clients are motivated to quit smoking when they start *making plans for the future* with their spouses, children, parents, and friends. This type of client knows that the moment they *make this change, they open up a* whole new world of possibilities for themselves, including a longer life!

I'm not sure which type of client you are, but I do know that it is very important to take some time to carefully consider all of the reasons *you want to quit*. Because we are communicating indirectly, through written text, you have the opportunity to *be your own best coach* throughout this process. So get a sheet of paper or open a file in your computer and make a list of all of *your* reasons for wanting to QUIT now. Pay close attention to the word now. Both you and I know that you are a smart person. You bought this book, which means for a good part of your life you've known that *smoking is bad for you* and that you need help stepping through the doorway into your new life where you have quit once and for all. What specifically is motivating you at this moment to *read this book* and QUIT? Be specific in your answers. Continue reading only after you have completely thought through all the reasons *you want to QUIT*.

The next question I am going to ask may sound strange at first. However, when you carefully consider it, you might discover something new. The question is this:

Once you have made this change, and that old habit is so far in the past that you barely even remember having it, how will you be different as a person from who you are now? How will you be feeling that is different? What will you be doing that you didn't do before quitting?

10

As you ponder this question, step into those amazingly *positive emotions that you will be feeling after you have become a healthy non-smoker*, whatever they may be for you. How will you be feeling about that old habit in your past when *you are free of cigarettes*? How will you be feeling about yourself, and the world around you, when you can simply *breathe more easily*?

You can even *make an image of yourself as a healthy non-smoker*, being this way and feeling great, knowing that *you have QUIT*. Make that picture big, bright, and colorful. Add motion to it so it is as though you're watching the best movie of your life. When you're ready, step inside the image and feel how good it feels to *be a healthy non-smoker*, to *be free*. Now step back out but keep this image with you. Let this be a driving motivation so you can *make this change easily*.

Take your time as you do this, and really build up the positive emotions. The questions above are not intellectual, and I do not expect an immediate answer. It is far more important for you to *get in touch with those good feelings* surrounding who you are becoming as a person.

At this point you may be wondering what this book will actually cover. Think of this book as if I were with you, personally coaching you, so *you can make this change with ease*. This book is a compilation of countless experiences in helping smokers just like you to QUIT. I will present the processes and techniques that have been shown time and time again to *help smokers QUIT successfully*.

Throughout the chapters you will have a number of experiences. Some will be centered around exercises, like this introduction. Others are intended to speak to you at a level beneath normal waking consciousness. I am, after all, a hypnotist, and therefore I will be speaking both to the conscious and your unconscious mind throughout this journey. In fact, as a hypnotist, I believe that the *best way to make changes is to involve your unconscious mind in the process*.

Think of it this way... You have both a conscious and an unconscious mind. Your conscious mind likes logic, whereas your unconscious mind likes stories. This is why children are expert learners; their unconscious minds are continuously engaged in storytelling. Stories are as old as humanity. Before the modern education system, the primary way people taught one another was through stories. There is a part of us that is deeply attracted to stories, and that is why stories are still so powerful. This is why you can see a film and be moved by emotions, or read a book that will *change your life*.

Your conscious mind likes words while your unconscious mind likes the sounds of words. Your conscious mind filters information and your unconscious mind learns easily. Your unconscious mind likes pure sensory experiences. This part of you likes to imagine and to try on new ideas and to have new feelings.

Because the best way to change is to *use both parts of your mind*, this book is designed to do just that. We will harness the ability of the conscious mind to follow procedures and strategies while it begins to speak the same language as your unconscious mind. Call to mind all of the things you consciously tried to quit smoking in the past. Consider also that they either only worked for a short period or didn't work at all. That was because you were using only half of your mind's capacity for change and growth. In reality the conscious mind has no business trying to make this change alone. It is the unconscious mind that learns, creates, and maintains habits. It is the unconscious mind that causes the change.

In fact, the reason you are still smoking up to reading this book is precisely because your unconscious mind believed that it was the best choice to make in the moment. It is not enough to consciously want to QUIT; it is also necessary to make your unconscious *fully understand the damage that smoking is doing to your health and well-being.* Once *your unconscious understands that smoking is bad for you*, that *smoking is dangerous and that there are other options available to you*, then *your unconscious can begin to make powerful changes.* Your unconscious can change the way you experience cigarettes, so that *cigarettes begin to taste foul and disgusting*, and *the more you smoke the worse they taste*. Your unconscious can change your experience so that even the *smell of cigarettes revolts you*.

And your unconscious can begin to *find healthier ways of dealing with the stresses* and boredom of everyday life.

How to Use This Book

Throughout this book you may find sentences that seem a little peculiar. Perhaps you have already noticed the abundance of italics. You can rest assured that these are *speaking to your unconscious mind about quitting*, because on the deepest level your *unconscious seeks to protect you from physical harm*. We are inviting your unconscious to take part. Understand that this book is designed to speak to both parts of you, so even when you think one thing is happening, know that you are right in assuming that there is much more occurring then you can consciously imagine at the moment. This is because no matter what you think you are at any moment, you are always so much greater than just that.

The best way to use this book both consciously and unconsciously is to follow the process step by step. If *you have already stopped smoking* then know you are well ahead and are moving in the perfect direction If you are still smoking as you start, then continue to smoke until you reach the point in the book when *you realize it is time to stop*.

As you consciously complete the exercises that follow, you can *allow your unconscious mind to absorb all of the learnings* taking place. There is no need to be caught up in wondering when exactly I am speaking to your conscious mind and when *I'm speaking to your unconscious*. Simply read this as you would any other book and enjoy the process. In fact the more you can *enjoy the process of changing* the easier and more automatic it becomes.

You will notice at the end of many chapters there are sets of exercises. These are divided into 2 categories: mind and body. Mind exercises are things you can do in your own mind to help the change process. Body exercises are physical activities for you to engage in as a part of your road to change.

The first time you read through this book please **read each chapter in order.** This book is designed to walk you through *easily quitting one step at a time.* These steps are meant to be completed in order just as my clients do when they quit smoking in my office. In the future feel free to come back to any part of the book to *refresh* your memory.

A Brief Introduction to Your Brain

It's not important for you to understand all of the ins and outs of your brain. As we go forward we will occasionally discuss the science behind quitting. Feel free to enjoy these neuroscience nuggets and perhaps you will discover even more ways to use your brain to make a change.

Inside of your head you have a wonderful mechanism called working memory. This is the user interface between all of the different parts of your brain and you. Working memory lets you know how to think, feel, and act. It determines how you understand the world around you and how you interact with it.

Working memory is comprised of three elements: a 3-second video loop, a sound track containing words and sounds, and finally a title. The video loop is constantly playing and represents a mixture of your current experience, memories, and thoughts about the future. The sound track can consist of any sounds contained in the movie, dialogue, or whatever sounds you choose to put in it, like music. The final and the most important part is the title of the movie. The title lets the brain know how to categorize the movie and how to act and feel in response.

To illustrate the structure and function of working memory, let me describe two of my clients. The first had a movie of herself in which she was acting fearlessly, which sounds great at first. But when the client and I explored this movie more deeply, we realized the title of that movie was, "I can't have this," as long as she held onto that title, she couldn't change; her brain was set in that pattern. However, as soon as we gave it a different title, things began to change. The second client had a movie of himself smoking at dinner. The title of his movie was, "That's the past; I'm different Now." This client changed quickly.

As you go through this book we will be presenting exercises and ideas that we encourage you to use. These will automatically engage your working memory and ensure that you have the movies, sounds, and titles that make *quitting cigarettes easy*.

A final word: the processes presented in this book mirror what we use with our clients who have successfully *quit smoking*. I understand that *you may quit immediately* as you start this process. Other people may take some time to *stop smoking* and for them it will take some practice. Still others will choose to *quit* the process, and continue breathing in *poison smoke*.

I don't know which type of person you will be. But if you are serious about *stopping this habit* and building a *bright healthy future* for yourself, then this *process will work for you* as well. Your success will be closely linked to your desire to *take control back* in your life. If you are not sure *you want to quit*, or if you do not feel the desire to *quit now*, then put this book down and come back when *you are truly ready to become smoke-free*.

Now that you're ready to *reclaim a healthy life* and to feel good knowing you set and achieved a goal that will extend your life, continue to the next chapter. And I would like to officially welcome you to your journey of transformation.

But before you go to the next chapter, make a special promise to yourself as you begin your journey. Take a few moments to make this commitment by filling in the information and promising yourself that *you are committed to creating a healthy future*.

Committed To Quitting

I am signing this today as my complete commitment to *become smoke free*. I promise myself to create and preserve this change in my life. I am building a new, healthy, and smoke free-life starting today as I begin my journey to becoming a non-smoker.

By the end of the process I promise to;
- Stop ingesting the toxic poisons found in cigarettes
- Stop causing emotional harm to myself because of smoking
- Stop poisoning those around me
- Stop being a slave to a company who profits from death

Instead I will:
- Reclaim my liberty to choose
- Value my health and well-being
- Start finding the importance of respecting myself and my body

As a result I will:
- Start feeling better and becoming healthier
- Respect those closest to me
- Start feeling good from the moment I wake up until I fall asleep and through my restful night
- Live the life I want to, free of old habits

I am fully committed to realizing my goal of being a non-smoker and know that I can achieve this. I make these promises to myself.

Signature
*Date*_____.

Chapter 2: The Cigarette Religion

You may think, "What an odd name for a chapter." But if you think about it, what does a religion consist of (beyond a description of the realm of the Divine)? On the level of an institution, religions consist of sets of tightly held beliefs that bind people to certain behaviors. In fact the word "religion" comes from Latin and means to bind. Until now, you have been a disciple of the Church of (Insert Cigarette Brand). What beliefs have you created about you, that habit and those cigarettes? What stories have you been telling yourself that in the past tied you to those things?

Our clients have shared a number of pretty standard beliefs. In fact, we fully expect every new smoking cessation client to have at least one or two of the beliefs we're about to describe. When you face these beliefs head on, you begin to undermine the foundation of the habit it supports.—It's like floodwater seeping into the foundation of an old abandoned building. With enough energy the building's structure is compromised and washed away. Once that old building has gone, the land is entirely clear so now you can *build something new*, beautiful, and useful.

We will spend some time on the most frequently encountered beliefs held by a client just starting their change process. Treat this chapter like a check-list and note which beliefs apply to you, and carefully consider how easy it might be to change that. Perhaps you have beliefs that are not listed here. If so, use the following discussion as an example of the things to consider, in order to *break free* of your own particular beliefs and be able to move forward. The second half of this chapter will present you with a set of empowering beliefs that you can adopt to help in the change process. Try those on and feel which beliefs are most helpful for you to change now.

Belief 1: I <u>Am</u> a Smoker

This idea was addressed in the previous chapter so I will only mention a few things here. The first is that you are not a smoker. Smoking is an activity not an identity. You are not a smoker when you are not lighting up. In fact you are not a smoker even when you do. Smokers are for cooking barbeque, they are not people.

Belief 2: I Have an Addiction

We are not doctors or psychologists and therefore we do not diagnose or call anything an addiction. If smoking were truly an addiction in the classical sense then common sense would lead one to believe that it's a long and hard process to quit. Our clients *know that this is simply not true*. If this were true it would be unlikely that our clients would *see dramatic change* so quickly. The sooner you *let go* of this idea of *addiction* the *easier* the whole process becomes. The idea of addiction is one of the most disempowering labels I come across in my coaching and hypnosis practice. Addiction implies that one is powerless to stop or be in control. With smoking that is simply not the case. You are in control.

Smoking is a habit. Nicotine stays in your system only for a few days. After that the chemical link is broken. This is not a chemical dependency issue but a habituated pattern. This is why some people successfully quit for a month, a year, or several years only to go back to the habit. It isn't the chemical that drives them back; it is caused by underlying emotional and behavioral factors.

Try this on for size…Stop for a moment and think to yourself, "I am addicted to cigarettes." How does that feel? Now say, "I have a cigarette habit." How does that feel? Which of those two statements is more empowering? I'm guessing you said the second statement. In which case, adopt that into your understanding of smoking: *it's just a habit, and one that is actually easy to break*. After all, it is you who has the habit and you who are *changing it now*.

Belief 3: Smoking Helps Me Relax/ Smoking is a Reward

If you are like many who hold this belief allow me to take a moment to congratulate you. This is in all sincerity. The fact that you believe this shows just how powerful your mind is. Nicotine essentially wages a war within your biochemistry. Within seven seconds of entering your body it activates the release of dopamine and serotonin two neurotransmitters related to feelings of reward and well-being. Next it activates the production of epinephrine, also known as adrenaline. This quickly elevates the heart rate, breathing, and blood pressure. It's the same chemical released when you feel the fight or flight response. Adrenaline is triggered in situations where there is a perceived fatal danger. Epinephrine is also used in conjunction with electrical shock to restart hearts. It's an incredibly potent chemical.

If you believe smoking makes you relaxed or is a reward, you should know that it is only because you have chosen to consciously pay attention to one half of the chemical reactions in your body. You are hallucinating away the rest of your biochemical responses.

If your brain can cancel an entire physiological response out of your awareness I wonder in what useful ways you can *use this* same ability. You might be curious about other times and places where it would be useful to *have an ability to cancel out bad feelings*. Or perhaps you can feel good in knowing that there are other organic ways of producing that dopamine, and other ways of feeling an even greater level of *relaxation* that is not possible with cigarettes.

Belief 4: It Won't Happen to Me

Everyone who smokes at some level holds the belief that all of the nasty side effects from smoking will not happen to them. If they didn't have this belief they wouldn't be smoking. The reality is that one in five deaths in the United States is due to smoking related causes every year. That is a tremendously high statistic; 20% of Americans die from smoking.

These odds are not too dissimilar from the following scenario. Suppose some shady person approached you in a dark alley. In their right hand was a revolver and in their left a bullet. They place the bullet into one of the chambers. They then hand you the gun and ask you to point it at yourself and pull the trigger. If you survive you get to give them $10 to try again the next time they come around. Our question to you is: how many times do you think you be willing to run a risk like that?

If you could see the risks as they really are, I doubt you would pick up the gun that first time. But the *cigarette* industry *is* hoping that you will ignore the facts and continue to play round after round of *Russian Roulette*. Eventually you will lose, but the cigarette companies still get paid.

Finally it has been discovered that smoking cigarettes actually changes your gene expression. That means the cigarette chemicals change your DNA. Cigarettes have been shown to turn off "good genes" and activate "bad genes" and more precisely the genes that make people vulnerable to not just cancer but also viruses and other infections, heart disease, and cigarettes impact cellular death. Cigarettes change DNA.

Belief 5: I'm Going to Die Anyway, May as Well Have Fun

This is an interesting belief because it is true we are all in fact going to die one day. The question is how do we want to go about it, and how long do we *want to live*. Death from smoking-related causes can be one of the most painful and degrading ways to exit this world. The question that we typically ask a client who holds this belief is whether they'd like to keep their lungs for the rest of their life or would they rather have them cut out piecemeal because they no longer function?

The next thing we ask our client is, "How long do you want to live?" Each cigarette you smoke steals ten minutes of your life from you. That is 10 minutes per cigarette. How many minutes have you shaved off your life today? How many minutes have you shaved off your life this year?

Think about it this way: because of smoking cigarettes, your family could one day get a call that they need to get to the hospital immediately if they want to speak to you one last time. But what if your family lives an hour away? If you'd smoked just six fewer cigarettes, they could have made it; twelve fewer and they could have spent an hour saying goodbye.

But if you QUIT *now*, you can give your family the *gift of years of extra healthy life* with them, time to see you kids graduate, your grandchildren born, your spouse and your friends grow old with you.

The good news is the moment you decide that you have had your last cigarette is the moment you begin to *extend your life*. Twenty minutes after *you have smoked your last cigarette* your blood pressure and heart rate begin to return to normal. Within eight hours the carbon monoxide levels in your blood also return to normal. In two days your body begins the process of repairing nerve endings and *your sense of taste and smell also begin to improve*. In the first 12 weeks your *breathing will improve* and walking will become easier. In the first nine months your lungs will have regained the ability to clean themselves. This means a decrease in the frequency of lung infections.

And then there are the truly life-changing benefits. After a year of being smoke-free, the *risk of coronary disease becomes half that of a smoker*. In the next five years your risk of stroke will become the same as someone who never smoked. You also will have cut the possibility of throat, mouth, and esophageal cancers in half. In the next decade your life expectancy will become that of someone who never smoked. Your body will also have the ability to replace precancerous cells with healthy ones. And in the next fifteen years the risk of heart disease will become the same as a person who never smoked cigarettes in the first place.

We get to choose how we spend the limited time we have on earth. The quality of our choices enables us to extend that precious time and, more importantly, to improve the quality of our time. How much time have you lost from the effects of cigarettes and the time spent buying and smoking them? How much time do you have to gain by *stopping now*?

Belief 6: I Can't Change

If you're like many of my clients, you have probably had the experience of quitting, only to break down and resume smoking at some point. Some people stop for a day and go back. Others stop for a couple weeks and go back. And still others hold out for months or even years before they pick up the habit again. Contrary to what you may think, it is really wonderful if you have had any of these experiences, because they all demonstrate that you have already experienced *quitting successfully*! Now you may be thinking, "Whoa, wait a minute; I went right back to smoking!" You're right; you did. But that doesn't diminish the value of your QUITTING in the past, however briefly; it simply emphasizes your need to practice the art of forgetting to start again. Small children often sleep with a plush toy, something that brings them comfort. You may have had one as a small child. Can you pinpoint the exact day when you stopped going to seep with that teddy bear? Odds are you may have a sense of sleeping with one at one age but not the next. At some point you realized on an unconscious level that you could be secure without it. Then you just forgot you needed the toy. You were sleeping easily and comfortably on your own. You didn't even give that toy another thought at bedtime.

All of the tools you used in the past are still useful today. The work we are doing now is simply to reinforce them with techniques that redirect your mind from smoking to something better. We're hoping to assist you in building on past achievements in order to experience permanent success.

On the other hand, this might be your first time quitting. If this is so, then allow us to show you an *easy path* to do it.

You really should know that *all you are is changing*. It's true! All we are is changing. Everything changes. The seasons change, ocean tides change, phases of the moon change. Even at this very moment you are changing at the cellular level. Who you were a year ago is distinctly different from who you are today. Over the course of the year, your body has disposed of old cells, *replacing them with new, young, healthy cells*. Over the past year, your knowledge has changed. What are all the things you learned in the past year that you did not know but you do now? Your memories have changed. You have spent the last year adding to and creating completely new memories. Your emotions and your feelings have fluctuated over this time.

In light of the fact that *everything about you is constantly changing*, how could you possibly believe that personal change is impossible? In fact it is impossible to halt change. Anyone who tells you they stay completely 100% the same is only deceiving herself. You are changing, and in the midst of this flux you can choose those aspects of yourself you want to change. That also means it gets to be *easy to change*. Since changing is your natural state, it takes far more work to remain stuck in a behavioral rut than it does to break free and follow a new and more productive path.

Resourceful Beliefs

If there were beliefs that made it difficult to change in the past, there must be beliefs that you can take on now that will make change easier. By focusing on such positive beliefs, you train your brain to search out events that support your objectives. Essentially, if you look for good things, you will find them. I suggest that you adopt beliefs that make it easier to make life changes. You can begin by just imagining what it would be like if you were to hold such beliefs. Imagine yourself as you would be if you truly believed you could change in certain ways. Then step into that you, acting and feeling as if *you hold these beliefs to be true* so that change is easy.

Belief 1: I Am A Successful Person.

You *are* a successful person. You wouldn't be reading this book now if you weren't. You had to be successful in order to *decide to quit* and have the money to purchase this book. Success has been with you your whole life. In fact you come from a long line of successful people over countless generations. Your ancient ancestors had to be successful at hunting, finding shelter, and finding spouses or you wouldn't be here now. Your background is filled with thousands of successful humans.

Of course, success breeds success. Successful people do not persist in doing unsuccessful things; they don't make the same mistake twice. They may have their setbacks, but when *you are successful,* you recognize those times and learn from them.

Success is not compartmentalized. Think about all of the times when you were being successful in life, and notice the images that come to mind. I wonder what it would be like if you were to take the energy and qualities of your successful interludes and compress them into a mental image of you *quitting for good.* How does this image make you feel that is different from before?

Belief 2: I Am in Control of My Feelings.

We know that this sounds strange at first, but it is actually true that no-one and nothing in the world can make you feel anything. No one has that much power over you. You get to decide how you feel. This is the reason why two people can experience the same circumstances and one person suffers while the other learns, grows, and overcomes. This belief is all about you stepping fully into the emotions that you want in life.

Whatever may have triggered smoking in the past is now changing. You get to choose your feelings. Neither life circumstances nor cigarettes can make you feel anything. You are in control and as you go on in this book you will be learning strategies that will help you to *take full control of how you feel*.

Belief 3: I Deserve to Be Healthy and Happy.

You do deserve these things and so much more! This belief is all about you getting in touch with that which is greater than you, with your purpose on this planet. We have a limited time here and we deserve to be happy and healthy. If we were to take a moment and really consider why we are here, what conclusion would we draw? Many people ascribe their existence to the Divine, whatever that means for them. Others may answer on a scientific basis. Either way is better.

How are you fulfilling your purpose? If you are religious or spiritual, you will know that happiness is a part of your right as a soul. If you are not religious, why not simply choose happiness and health? Out of a vast and infinite universe you came into existence. Make the most of it!

Of course with happiness comes responsibility. You are responsible for your body, the form that allows you to experience the world in ways that bring happiness. You have a responsibility to protecting this perfect machine that is your body.

Belief 4: I Am Flexible in My Behaviors, Feelings, and Thoughts.

When you were younger you did things that you no longer do. You may, for example, have played a game as a child that you now wonder how you could ever have found enjoyable. Behaviors change over time. Some preferences change completely unconsciously. You may not remember the exact moment when you became "too old" for that game; it just kind of happened. Other behaviors change because you decide it is time to *do something different*.

The very same thing is true about your feelings and thoughts. They change over time whether you choose to change them or they change on their own. The more thoughts and feelings you choose to change, the more you will be actively in control of your life.

Flexibility also means patience. In the middle of a hurricane a mighty oak topples in the wind while the palm tree bends with the wind, returning to normal once the atmosphere calms. Life doesn't always go according to our plans. The trick is to remember that *you can be flexible*. When things don't go the way you wanted them to, you need to have the flexibility to *reset and start over*.

This is the difference between a person who has one cigarette and thinks they are a failure, a smoker again, and the person who thinks and feels, "well that happened, but it was just one moment in my whole life and, once more, I am choosing to think, feel, and *be different*."

Going forward, I am curious how easily you can change as you carry these new, empowering, and transformative beliefs not only to QUIT smoking but also to accomplish other self-transformative objectives in other areas of your life.

Chapter 3: Let's Get Real

When we first developed our protocol to help people kick the habit we used something called "aversion techniques". This approach was motivated by the school of aversion therapy. The basic approach was to link revolting imagery to the behavior that was targeted for elimination.

In applying this therapy, we would, for example, invite clients to *imagine that the ingredients of cigarettes included the nastiest things possible.* We encouraged clients to *picture dirt from the subway, animal feces, dumpster juice,* and other things no sane person could possibly *imagine putting in your mouth.*

We no longer engage in such revolting imagery because the truth behind what is actually in cigarettes is far worse.

Imagine for a moment you invite someone into your home who you consider to be your friend. Imagine that you have known them for a very long time. As a good host, you fix her something to drink. As you both sit down, your phone rings, and you excuse yourself to answer the call. While you're away, your friend pours *battery acid* into your drink. When you return you take a sip. After talking for a few moments you go to the kitchen to get her something to eat. While you're gone, she dumps *lighter fluid* into the very same drink. You return to your drink only to be called away again, and this time that friend dropped *nail polish remover* and paint into your drink. This time when you return you notice a funny smell coming from your drink so you leave it sitting on your table. This friend of yours sitting right in front of you then proceeds to pull out a bottle of *arsenic* and sprinkles it into your drink. The "friend" proceeds to top off your drink with lighter fluid, insecticide, and toilet bowl cleaner. Yuck.

Two questions for you: would you drink the concoction? And is that person your friend?

Because you most likely answered "no" to these questions, how is it that you have been able to ignore the fact that the tobacco industry is doing exactly the same thing to you? Think about it. The ingredients of the cigarette include nicotine (insecticide), cadmium (batteries), arsenic, stearic acid (candle wax), toluene (industrial solvent), ammonia (toilet bowl cleaner), methane (sewer gas), acetone (nail polish remover), to name a few of the chemicals

When you're ready to *consider on a deeper level exactly what you've been ingesting*, pull a cigarette out of your pack now, and hold it as you normally do if you were smoking. As you do so, consider what it would be like to ingest each one of those chemicals one at a time.

As you're holding the cigarette, imagine the smell and taste of bleach. Imagine the stench of methane gas. Imagine tipping a car battery into your mouth. And you no longer need to imagine you are drinking insecticide and eating arsenic, because you know now what is actually in that cigarette!

Of course this is only half the story. Let's take a moment to explore how expensive smoking is. Put this book down and go grab a calculator. What is the price of cigarettes for you per day? Are you a half a pack a day smoker, a pack a day smoker, a two-pack-a-day smoker? Calculate how much you spend on cigarettes a day.

Multiply that by seven and discover how much you're spending a week. Take that amount and multiply it by four to see the number of dollars you're burning each month. Now multiply that by 12 and you will get the exact *cash amount that you've burnt over the past year*. For example, if someone is a pack a day smoker and their cigarettes cost seven dollars a pack, they lose $49 a week. Each month they throw away $196. And finally $2,352 a year is set on the funeral pyre. You could take it a step further and find out how much you've lost over the amount of time you've been smoking, if *you're brave enough to look at that*. Once you've calculated *how much money you're wasting*, imagine taking the actual dollar bills and setting fire to them, *watching your hard earned money go up in smoke*.

We can, of course, extend this analysis quite a bit further. The economic impact of smoking is far larger than just the cost of the cigarettes. Other expenses are tied to this habit as well. Count into the cost of smoking the money paid for lighters and matches, dry cleaning to get the smell out of your clothes, steam cleaning to get the stench out of your carpeting, and so on. Of course all of this is loose change compared to healthcare costs. Health insurance companies in the U.S. are legally permitted to charge smokers up to 50% more on their monthly premiums. A nonsmoker could have a health plan that charges them $200 per month, while a smoker with the same plan would end up paying $300 per month. Thus, over a year, the smoker pays $3600, or $1200 more than the non-smoker with the same plan. Added to the cost of cigarettes, our smoker is so far out $5900 a year for his habit.

This of course is on a healthy year. Smoking will lead to health issues that will raise the price much, much more. One study found that smokers average about 11 more sick days a year than non-smokers. How much money will you lose with 11 extra sick days? Whatever figure you might compute, it is nothing compared to the cost of a lung transplant. Transplants begin at around half million dollars per lung. And to receive that lung you will be required to quit smoking anyway.

For now let's bring the economic impact back to just the money you are spending right at this moment. We wonder just what you would do with the money, with that extra $5900 a year. Would you take a vacation or maybe treat yourself to something special? Or perhaps you'd invest it to grow your wealth. Take a moment to dream about what you can do with that extra money you will be saving as a non-smoker. Over the rest of your life, how much money do you think you might save by giving up that habit right now? Without a doubt, you'll be *saving tens of thousands of dollars;* over a couple of decades and factoring in health insurance and modestly increased health problems, it is not unreasonable to estimate a loss of *hundreds of thousands of dollars.* That is a tremendous amount of extra wealth you get to accrue simply by making this change and deciding to QUIT *now.*

Chapter 4: Tracking Your Habit

Every habit is associated with certain things in the environment that trigger it. Triggers might consist of certain things we see, hear, or touch that lead to the behavior. Having a clear understanding of what those particular triggers are for you will make it *very easy to make this change* and QUIT *now*.

For people who smoke there are two types of triggers that lead to the behavior. The first type are environmental stimuli that set off the behavior automatically. For example, some smokers may see their cup of coffee and automatically reach for the cigarettes. Or perhaps they see that it's 10:30 a.m., which means it's time for the cigarette break. Still others may only need to see a pack of cigarettes to be compelled to reach for them. When you realize which automatic triggers apply to you, it is time to *stop being a slave and take back your freedom.*

The second type of trigger is emotional. These are things that happen in our environment that create certain emotions that ignite the craving for a cigarette. An example of an emotional trigger might be the sound of our boss's voice, which makes you feel anxious – and in need of a smoke. Indeed, the most common type of emotional triggers are linked to stress or anxiety. In the next chapter we will show you some ways to *deal with these stresses easily* and *feel more relaxed.*

Smokers respond to both types of triggers. If you consider your day-to-day smoking habits you will find both automatic triggers as well as emotional triggers. The next exercise will help you become much more familiar with the situations that make you reach for a pack of cigarettes.

Get a sheet of paper (or use the chart at the end of this chapter) and create a timetable with four columns. On the left-hand side of the paper, in the first column, list all of the hours you are awake, starting with the time you wake up in the morning. For the purpose of this exercise you can use yesterday as your model. Next to each time indicate how many cigarettes you smoked in that hour. Next to that write down what was happening to let you know it was time to smoke. What is it you are seeing and hearing that let you know it is time to smoke? Are you, for example, eating breakfast in your kitchen, smelling the coffee, and seeing the cigarette pack? In the last column indicate what emotions you are feeling right before you reach for that cigarette.

Doing this exercise will give you a picture of your own smoking pattern throughout the day. It will become clear what activities and what emotions lead to the smoking behavior. Keep this sheet; we will use it in the next chapter.

So far we've laid the foundations for you to QUIT completely. You've made a list of specific reasons for you as to why this change is important. You have also stepped into the future and discovered just how good it will feel when this behavior is so far in the past you no longer remember even having the problem. We've also explored some of the beliefs or excuses people have for not quitting, and you've had the opportunity to consider how you can overcome any limiting beliefs you've placed on yourself. And finally we looked at the reality of what cigarettes are for you on a physical and emotional level.

Time	Number of Cigarettes	How Do You Know it's Time to Start Smoking?	Emotions

Chapter 5: Trading Triggers

One of the unconscious mind-tricks smokers use to get themselves to smoke is to place themselves inside the cigarette. They step inside and imagine how good it will feel to smoke. Now I know this sounds strange, but think about it: how else could that cigarette be so attractive unless you placed part of yourself inside it? Maybe you placed your hopes for relaxation into it. Or perhaps it was the need to rebel that the teenage you placed in that cigarettes. It's like you've been putting some part of yourself into that cigarette and then dragging the rest of you kicking and screaming toward the cigarette until you reached out for it.

Given all of the awful things in cigarettes, let's not forget the rat poison, what a terrible place to put part of your awareness. Why not *shift your awareness to something else*, anything else. If, for example, you should find yourself being pulled toward a cigarette, stop and ask yourself, "What's everything else other than that that I can be paying attention to now?" I know this sentence is awkward to the conscious mind however it is purposefully designed that way. Try it out and notice what happens. Because you could also think about the last time and place you really wanted a cigarette and considered, "What is everything else that I haven't been paying attention to now, that could *bring me closer to the life I want for myself?"*

There are many places in which you can put your attention. You could *put your attention in anything else in your surrounding environment.* Or you could *create for yourself something wonderful*, so attractive that you forget all about the cigarettes, as you *become enthralled with the idea of who you are becoming.*

We had a client once who found herself drawn to smoking when she saw her full coffee mug, or the color on the pack of cigarettes, or her work computer. If she didn't see those things, she didn't feel that compulsion. It was very clear that something in her visual system was firing off the smoking response. This was great news as something like this is very easy to change. We are not sure what kind of triggers are in your environment, but you could *call them to mind now.*

Start with one specific trigger. For one client it was the color on their cigarette box; for you it is probably something else entirely. Maybe you're thinking about your first cigarette of the day, which starts by seeing the alarm clock, the cup of coffee, the lighter, or something else specific.

I said to her, *"Choose one specific instance,* one thing in your environment that triggers your desire to smoke. Now let that image drift to one side for the moment. Now I would like you to make an image of yourself being the person you want to become, now that *"you've* QUIT *smoking."* So of course she creates the image of the ideal self. You know what it's like when you daydream and *paint a picture in your mind of who you want to be.* "Why not add in all the best qualities you want in yourself," I asked her.

"The next step is to take that ideal picture and, for the time being, shrink it down to the size of the postage stamp and place it right in the middle of that first picture of what you see right before you smoke. Now in a moment, but not yet, I'm going to ask you to send that combo picture (the trigger plus your ideal self) far away, out in the distance, making it smaller and smaller the further away it goes.

Once it is as far as it will go, it will snap back as if it's on a rubber band. However, it is going to come back as the picture of the ideal you, becoming closer and larger and replacing the old picture, so the only thing that you see coming back is that ideal you," I suggested to the client.

Once the client indicated the new picture had come back, I said, "Now, blank the screen; in other words, clear the image from your mind. Now repeat the process. See the picture of the trigger, shoot it off into the distance and have it come back as the ideal you as fast as possible now." We did this five times together. She took the old trigger picture and placed that postage-stamp-sized picture of the ideal you on it and send it out into the distance. When the picture snapped back, it was transformed into her ideal self. She then blanked the screen and repeated the process. She then did this five times on her own without me guiding her.

To her delight she discovered that *the old triggers had changed.* "Now they only remind you of who you are becoming," I said.

If you remember, at the beginning of our journey I asked you to write down the different things that you saw and heard before you used to smoke. This step will be all about neutralizing those things in your external experience that led to smoking in the past. This strategy will allow you to take what once caused you trouble, and transform it into a trigger for excellence. As we go through the steps of this process, I cannot encourage you enough to put as much energy and emotion into it as possible.

Let's begin. Take a moment and imagine that ideal you. Form a picture in your mind of the person you are becoming now that smoking is no longer part of your life. Become aware of how healthy you look. You can even notice the type of positive emotion you have in this image. Consider how you will be as a person once smoking is so far in your past it's no longer a part of you. You could think about all of the things you won't be doing, won't be feeling, and will not be smelling. However, it can be far more powerful to *consider all of the things you __will__ be doing, feeling, and smelling.*

Make this image of you big, bright and glowing. Make the "you" in the image so incredibly compelling that you know that *you want to be that*. This means you can make that "you" in that picture exactly how you want to be, physically, emotionally, and spiritually. You can give this image any quality that you want for yourself, and make it so compelling that you just feel it. The picture should make you lick your lips and think, "Yes, *I want this now.*"

Now do the exercise we described above. Imagine you can shrink the picture of the ideal you down to the size of a postage stamp. Take one of the triggers that used to make you want to smoke, and imagine placing the postage stamp on it. Now imagine the trigger flying off into the distance… and when it returns it comes back as the ideal you, but this time big, bright, and life sized. Now, blank the screen; see the trigger again, and repeat, sending it into the distance then coming back as the ideal you, big and bright. Repeat until *every time you see the trigger, you will automatically see the ideal you.*

Repeat this with all the triggers you can think off.

As you see that ideal you, if you could give that image a one- word title, what would it be? If you could use one word to sum up the emotional power of that image, what is that word? When that word comes to mind write it down.

If you could give that feeling a symbol, what would that be? What 'you' fully and completely represents this version of you that you are becoming? Once you have that symbol draw it.

Now take a moment to consider how this word and the symbol represent who you will be once you have fully made this change. Attached to these two things are all of the emotions that propel you forward to achieve this outcome.

It's time to attach these good feelings to those things that triggered smoking in the past. Get a piece of paper or some post-its, and write that word and draw the symbol that represent the you that you're becoming now. As you do this, take the time to really put your emotions into the word and pictures

Take these pieces of paper and stick them to all of the items in your environment that used to trigger smoking. This could be a pack of cigarettes, the computer screen, maybe a coffee mug. Attach the papers to the items you would see right before you used to light up a cigarette. Each time you see a post-it take a moment to connect to all of the good feelings and the identity represented on last sheet.

Moving Forward

So now is the time to take the leap. If you haven't stopped smoking yet, *smoke your last cigarette tonight* and do not smoke tomorrow. When you have time tomorrow, pick up this book and continue on your journey. This step is important. Do not read on until *you have smoked your absolute last cigarette* and it has been at least eight hours since you smoked it. Make this commitment to yourself so that you can enjoy the ease of success that is waiting for you in the next chapters.

Mind Exercise Steps

1. Think about one of the instances you smoke and notice what specifically in your environment you are seeing as you feel the need to reach for the cigarettes

2. Push that image to the side for the moment.

3. Create an image of the ideal you who is smoke free, health and happy. The secret here is to build up your good emotions around that image and really feel you want it.

4. Shrink the image of the ideal you down to the size of a postage stamp. We will make it big again in a moment, we promise.

5. Bring back image 1 (the trigger for smoking) and place image 2 (the postage stamp) in the center of that image.

6. Send the new image quickly out into the distance so it gets smaller and smaller until you can no longer see it.

7. Way out in the distance the image changes and the new you image is big and bright as it comes back right in front of you. Make this image larger than life and feel the excitement of knowing this is who you are becoming at this moment.

8. Blank the screen.

9. Repeat several times quickly so that when you see or think of that old trigger you see that new you flash into your mind. Remember to blank the screen between each round.

Body Exercise

1. Make a picture again of that future you who is free and enjoying life. What word comes to mind to represent this?

2. If you could give this word a symbol to represent who you are becoming, what would that be?

3. Get pieces of paper or sticky notes and write the word and draw the symbol on that paper.

4. Take those sticky notes and post them to every trigger in your environment including coffee cups, packs of cigarettes, the steering wheel of your car and/or anything else that used to remind you to smoke.

Chapter 6: Breaking Through Cravings

As we begin, we would like to congratulate you for *making the commitment to yourself* to QUIT. If you followed the instructions in the last chapter, it has been at least eight hours since *you smoked your last cigarette.* Think of all of the wonderful changes that are happening in your body because of that. Carbon monoxide levels are falling. Your heart rate and blood pressure are returning to normal. All of this happened as you slept last night. So feel good in knowing that *you have already* QUIT. You are already a non-smoker. Not only that but you are at least *eight hours into being a non-smoker.*

We recognize that some readers may be experiencing certain feelings and sensations in the body connected to not smoking. This is normal considering you are making such an important *change for the better*. In the next few chapters we are going to be focusing on strategies and techniques that you can use at any place and any time to *overcome cravings and deal with any negative emotion* you may be experiencing.

Something useful to keep in mind as you continue on is that cravings are emotions, and emotions are just the labels we give to sensations in the body. The interesting thing is that *an emotion only lasts about 90 seconds.* That is the amount of time it takes for the neurotransmitters in your brain to communicate a signal to your glands to release a hormone that creates the sensation you call an emotion. It takes 90 seconds for that chemical wash to go through your system. If an emotion lasts longer than 90 seconds, you are doing something in your head to keep it going. You could be making pictures, experiencing memories, or talking about it in your mind.

This is fantastic news because if you're using your mind to maintain a sensation for longer than 90 seconds, with less resourceful emotions you can just wait out the 90 seconds and *be done with them; they're gone.* This is true whether we are talking about the cravings of the cigarette or about emotions that would lead a person to smoke, for example stress. But the great news is that you can stretch out really fantastic feelings for as long as you want. The techniques presented here can be used directly with the cravings or with any emotion that in the past would have led you to smoke.

To begin we are going to introduce a four-step process that will help to clear the space in between you and a craving. This process is not our own but comes from renowned researcher in obsessive-compulsive disorders, Dr. Jeffrey Schwartz. This technique is so powerful that when he taught it to his OCD clients, over a period of time their brains exhibited the same healing changes as those people who had been on prescription drugs. When used to treat OCD, Dr. Schwartz administers his treatment in a series of 15 minute sessions over a considerable period. But while a prolonged treatment time may be necessary for OCD, we can use the same procedures over a far shorter period to *let go of cravings.* Of course if you find that a longer treatment time results in a higher rate of improvement for you please feel free to move at your own rate.

This *technique is powerful* and elegant in its simplicity. I encourage you to use it whenever you feel a craving starting. It will loosen your attachment to the feelings and put you into a calm frame of mind where you can create changes in your physiology. Think of it this way: if this treatment changes the brains of people with medically diagnosed issues, how much easier will it be to use it to break a habit?

The technique has four easy steps.

Step 1: Re-label

When a craving begins, it's important to recognize it for what it is. Someone who isn't interested in quitting will experience a craving as it moves through the body as a stress response. They have to have a cigarette. They think that if they don't get the cigarette the feeling will get worse. We know that's not actually true. When you acknowledge the feeling and just let it go, it will subside in about 90 seconds. Nothing bad has ever happened to someone who refused to have another cigarette.

Because *you are ready* to QUIT and you understand the 90 second rule, *this step will be easy*. Recognize the feelings for what they are. Give them a label. The easiest way to do this is to recognize that the cravings are actually sensations in the body and thoughts in the mind. Bring mindfulness to it. It's not enough to have a normal awareness that you are experiencing cravings. With this step you bring a deep mindfulness to the experience by saying something to yourself like, "I am experiencing sensations in my body and I'm having thoughts in my mind."

Step 2: Reattribute

In this step we expand the separation between you and those thoughts and sensations. At this point it's time to recognize these feelings and thoughts for what they actually are. In the past you weren't sure *you can escape them* or whether *you can control them*. In reality *you are in control* because *neither the feelings nor the thoughts are you*.

Let's take a brief look at what is actually happening when you have those cravings. Inside of your body you have a natural feel-good drug called dopamine. Dopamine does a number of very important things in the body and we will look at it more in the next few steps. For now simply keep in mind that this drug is released in the part of your brain connected with reward and motivation. When someone is craving cigarettes, it is these same parts of the brain that are active.

The fascinating thing is, studies have shown that by activating the prefrontal cortex, your logic center, you can *deactivate the reward and motivation response*. This means in your neurology you can actually stop the part of your brain that in the past produced cravings from making new cravings. We're going to do this step by using the part of your brain that can think things through logically. And you can do this very easily when *you put the craving into its proper context*.

You put the craving in it proper context by recognizing that the feelings and sensations are not you, they are simply brain activity brought on by repetitive behavior. So when you feel a craving, STOP and bring mindfulness to the moment by thinking or saying to yourself, "I am experiencing sensations and thoughts. These are not me. They are only brain activity brought on by repetitive behavior."

Step Three: Refocus

In Schwartz's model this step entails doing something different. After recognizing the sensations and feelings and seeing them for what they are, it's time to put your attention on something else. In this case you are going to be shifting your attention to activities that increase dopamine.

Dopamine is in charge of creating good feelings. In fact it's a bit of a continuous cycle. When you feel good your body produces dopamine when your body produces dopamine you feel good. Dopamine is what allows you to learn and is what gives you that great feeling when something is better than you expected.

Nicotine is often referred to as a dopamine imposter. In your brain, nicotine attaches to the neural receptors intended for dopamine. What's more, nicotine causes a dilation of the blood cells, which means it, and all of the other poisons in the cigarettes, are transported throughout the body more quickly and easily. Nicotine also diminishes the production of dopamine in your body. It essentially tricks your brain while poisoning your body.

The good news is that this state doesn't have to be permanent. In fact you can naturally increase your body's production of dopamine, which means that you can train your brain to make you feel good on its own. By doing this you teach the brain to reactivate dopamine production. After the nicotine has been out of your system for a few days, the dopamine you are now producing will have clean receptors to attach to.

One of the quickest ways to stimulate dopamine production is to introduce novel experiences, that is to say, do something new! The techniques you are about to learn will create novel experiences in your mind and thus produce the "feel good" drug. These techniques also use your brain in a way that physiologically diminishes the sensation of cravings. You can think of these techniques as being both craving busters and dopamine producers, a wonderful two-for-one! The more you practice them the better you will feel, and the easier it will be to let go of that old habit. After all, it's far better to feel good whenever you want to, without having to be a slave to poison. In the next two chapters you will learn two of the quickest and most effective techniques for accomplishing this: the Backward Spin, and Emotional Freedom Techniques (EFT).

Step Four: Revalue

The first three steps were geared towards letting go of the feelings of craving a cigarette. This simply means creating the space for you to step back and see that the cravings are not what you first thought they were. By the time you reach this fourth step, you are already experiencing the ways in which you can *take charge of your feelings and begin to change them*. Ultimately those sensations and thoughts begin inside of you, which means you create them and therefore have control over them.

Once you have a number of experiences using the three steps above, including using the backward spin and EFT in step three (we will describe these techniques in the following chapters), something will begin to shift inside of you. This change begins to reframe the entire experience of the craving. It is no longer something that's outside of your control and overpowering but instead is an opportunity for you to use your brain in a new way. It is the moment where you get to *take full control of how you think and how you feel*. When you do this, the craving dies. It loses its energy. Remember: where your attention goes, your energy flows. You have redirected your attention to things that are of more value and more importance to you, which means that the cravings become less and less important until they reach the point where they are no longer worth even being in your awareness.

As you read the next two chapters keep these four steps in mind. Remember to add in one or both of the following techniques into step three. These two techniques will not only refocus your attention but they actually change the way in which your brain processes information about that craving. You are using your biochemistry to transform yourself, transitioning from a person with an old habit to someone who has *reclaimed freedom*.

Mind+ Body Exercise

1. Re-label the craving as a sensation in your body. Do not judge it.

2. Recognize the sensation for what it is, a wash of biochemicals that is washing through your system for a brief period of time.

3. Do something different. Use the techniques in the subsequent chapters to feel differently.

4. Revalue the experience as an exercise in using your brain in a new way.

Chapter 7: The Backward Spin

The first technique to eliminate cravings is called the backward spin. To do this you will need to be in touch with the physical sensations of the craving. If you are not craving a cigarette right now you have three choices. You can make yourself crave one, which after all you have lots of experience doing in the past, and use the backward spin to transform it. You can wait until a craving appears, before you continue to read on. Or you can continue reading knowing that this information is here if you should need it in the future. You may find that if you choose the second or third option you may not even need to turn back to these pages. You can comfortably rest assured that they are here should you need them.

There are two types of emotions we tend to experience as humans. The first is a fast moving one, an emotion that starts in one place and then leaves, it kind of jumps outside you. An example of this would be the experience of a sudden loud noise when you aren't expecting it. This startling feeling starts in one part of the body, maybe the stomach or chest, and moves up and out. The body will show this with a slight jump, or scream, or sharp inhale or exhale.

The second type of emotion is one that lingers. It cycles through the body over and over again. Someone who experiences worry or stress has a lot of experience with this type of emotion. A craving is this type of emotion. It keeps cycling through the body until you do something about it. The good news is there are many things you can do aside from smoking that will change the experience. Think of it this way: when you have an emotion that cycles through your body, then the same sets of neurons are firing over and over again in your brain. If you engage a different set of neurons, it changes the way the original set is firing. This means that the experience in the body has changed, it cannot stay the same. You are interrupting an unresourceful process with something far more resourceful.

The exercise we will do here does exactly this. It introduces new information and causes the experience in the body to reverse itself.

The first step of this is very simple. When you have the craving, notice the sensation of the craving in your body. Become aware of where that sensation starts for you. Some people notice it first in their head or throat, for others it begins in their chest or some other part of the body. Just notice where it starts for you. Once you sense it, become aware of where the feeling travels to next. After that, where does it go? Does it move to another location? How many places does the sensation go before it cycles back to its starting point and begins the sequence all over again?

As you notice the movement of the feeling, begin to trace it with your hand. Keep your hand moving in that way for now.

As you trace the motion of the craving, focus on how fast or slow the feeling is moving. Maybe this feeling even has a temperature or texture. Does that feeling have a color? If it doesn't and you could give it a color, what color would you give it? Spend a few moments becoming familiar with all of the different qualities of the sensation as it travels through your body. Your only job at this point is to be mindful of the experience.

Now, imagine you can pull that feeling outside of you. Take your hand that is tracing the path of the craving and move it further away from your body, so you can literally see the craving moving outside your body, in the space just in front of you. Notice its size, see its color, and be aware of its speed and direction. Once you have a sense of its direction, reverse its direction. Begin to move your hand in the opposite direction to track it. Watch it as it flows differently. Once you've done that, begin to change the speed. Slow it down or speed it up to a rate that feels more comfortable. Feel what happens as you watch that feeling out there going the opposite way.

If you want, you can change the size of the loop it is making to a size that is more comfortable. Or maybe change the temperature or the color of the feeling. What color would represent relaxation or comfort for you? Change the feeling into that new color. Spend a few moments to feel the shifts in your own body as you change that sensation out there in front of you.

If you would like you can take that sensation and turn it on its side so you see it from a completely different orientation. If that makes you feel more relaxed, keep it that way. If not, then flip it back. It is time to playfully experiment with the shape, direction, speed, size, color, temperature, and so on, so that the feeling is perfect for you. And when you're ready, and you are sure that all of the different changes have been made so that qualities of that sensation in front of you are more comforting and relaxing, you can pull this new feeling back inside you and feel how things are different now.

You can repeat this process as many times as it takes for the feeling to subside, or to be transformed into something new. Many people find that the first time through creates the change. Each time you do the backward spin process, you change the qualities of the emotion into something new. There is no need to go back to the old feeling. Always start from where you are now.

The backward spin works with any emotion that cycles through the body. You can use this on cravings, but you can also use it on any emotion that in the past would have led you to smoking. If you look on your sheet describing when and where you used to smoke, you will find the different emotions that you experienced throughout your day that contributed to that old behavior. You can send each one of those feelings in the opposite direction and create new productive sensations. In fact, the next time you feel one of those nagging sensations use this exercise and enjoy experiencing the change that can happen deep inside you.

Consider this to be the first of many ways *you can directly and positively impact how you feel*. This isn't just about stopping an old habit; this is about *taking control and creating responsibility in your life for how you feel*. In coaching this is called "being at cause." The more often you make yourself at cause, responsible for how you feel, the easier and quicker it is to change so that you can be feeling more of the emotions that are useful to you. As you continue reading the remaining chapters you'll be invited both consciously and unconsciously to be at cause for how you feel, for your actions, and for your change. And as my friend John Overdurf says, you never know how far the change will go.

Mind Exercise

1. Notice emotion in the body and track it. In your mind be aware of where it starts, where it goes to next, and when does it loop back to the starting point.

2. Pull the feeling outside of your so that you can see it spinning.

3. Make it go the opposite way.

4. Change the speed, texture, temperature, and orientation of the loop until it is more comfortable.

5. Change the color of the emotion to something more relaxing for you.

6. Pull the new feeling back into you.

Chapter 8: Emotional Freedom Techniques

Continuing with the theme of taking control of your emotions and controlling your cravings, we will now discuss one of the most powerful self-hypnosis techniques I know, the Emotional Freedom Techniques (EFT) first developed by Gary Craig. In fact this technique is so powerful that not only do I teach it to all of my clients, I use it myself. I once had a client who was nearly completely deaf which made it nearly impossible to use a traditional hypnosis approach with her. I decided to teach her EFT instead. It was the only process we used for the entirety of our two-hour session. By the end of those two hours, the client threw out her pack of cigarettes and told me she was completely finished with smoking. She had the opportunity to come back for a follow up but emailed me before her session to cancel. She didn't need it as she hadn't smoked, and never wanted to again! That is how transformative this process can be.

At first EFT looks a bit strange, but that is to be expected because this is a book written hypnotists, and a good many of the things hypnotists do seem strange at first. It seems far stranger to me though to light a fire next to your face so you can breathe in the fumes and damage your health in dozens of ways!

Keep in mind that one of the things your brain loves is novelty. In fact novelty releases dopamine in the brain, and dopamine facilitates learning. So the more strange and novel the experience, the more dopamine you release, the better you feel, and the easier it is to learn something new.

EFT is based on the fact that we carry emotions in our body. We know this to be true; when someone feels stress it results in tension in the muscles. This means that we can also use the body to change our emotional state. EFT uses the same principles as acupressure; specifically, it describes how you can *tap on certain points on the body to release negative energy* and *transform emotions*.

Let's take a moment to consider the different points of the body we use for this process. On the next page you will find a diagram of these points.

It's important to remember that our goal is to release emotion. There is no correlation between the strength of the tapping and the release of the emotion. So be gentle and kind to yourself.

Before we begin the process of releasing emotions, we will do a dry run by simply tapping on the points. It doesn't matter which side of the body you select. You may choose to tap with your right hand if you are right-handed, but whichever side you choose to *begin to release those emotions is fine*. You may even discover that you enjoy tapping on both sides at the same time.

Start by tapping on the outside of either hand, just along the side of the hand below the little finger. This is called the karate-chop point.

Next we move to the top of the head, the crown. You may want to use the flat of your hand to gently tap on this point.

Next we move to the inner corner of the eyebrow followed by the outer corner of the eye near the temple. From there we move to the point just below the eye, right around the cheekbone.

The next point is the cleft just under the nose, between your nose and your upper lip. We follow that with the point just below your lower lip on your chin.

We now leave the face and tap on a point just over your heart on the sternum. Alternately some people like to tap on a point just under the collar-bone, but either will *work equally well for releasing negative emotions*.

From there you go to the spot underneath the arm on your ribs, at a level that is aligned with the nipple. For ladies this will be along your bra line. The final point is on the inside of the wrist near the palm.

With the exception of the first point on hand and the last point on the wrist, we cycle through all of these points a number of times. When we begin the process of EFT we start on the hand, and only when these cycles are completely finished do we tap on the wrist near the palm.

Tapping in and of itself has a very nice calming effect. But we are going to *add additional power* by adding statements that you can repeat during the process to create transformation.

To get in touch with your negative emotion, you can name it anything that is appropriate for you. If you smoke when you feel stressed, or bored, you would say, "…this stress…", or, "…this boredom…" Now rate the emotion on a scale of one to ten, with ten being the strongest. This will give you a way of deciding later how much *the feeling has diminished*.

I like to cycle through the statement three times on the karate-chop point on the side of the hand. These statements follow a very simple formula. We start on the hand and repeat as follows:

"Even though I feel this (state your emotion, for example "this craving"), *I still deeply and completely love and accept myself."* (Repeat this three times).

Now we begin to tap the points in order whilst acknowledging the negative emotion and changing it.

For example:

Top of the head: *"This craving".*
Inner corner of the eyebrow: *"this craving".*
Outer eye near the temple: *"this craving".*
Under the eye: *"that craving".*
Under the nose: *"I choose to let it go".*
Under the lip: *"It is no longer useful to me".*

Now when you move to the heart you get to choose to feel differently. As you tap repeat to yourself,

Heart/sternum: *"In its place I choose to feel* (choose a good emotion, for example "relaxation")".

Under the arm: *"relaxation"*

You may also choose to continue tapping on the various points to build up the positive state.

Once you cycle through two or three times and have experienced a change in state, move to the wrist and simply take a deep, refreshing breath.

These statements might flow something like this:

"Even though I feel this craving I still completely and deeply love and accept myself.
Even though I feel this craving.
This craving.
That craving.
I choose to let it go.

*It is no longer useful.
In its place I choose to feel relaxed.
I choose to feel relaxed.
I am choosing to feel relaxed
I am relaxing
I am relaxed"*

It generally takes about two rounds to *diminish the craving completely*. Have a go at this and *enjoy releasing and transforming your emotions. Have fun tapping and talking*, whatever you do *will work just fine*.

The great thing is this isn't only applicable to smoking. You can use it in other parts of your life to have greater freedom. In fact if you look on your sheet of paper you may find some emotions that in the past led you to smoking. Choose one of those emotions and remember the last time and place you experienced it. Be precise: one time and one place. The easiest way to change is one step at a time, and that is exactly what we are doing here.

Step into that last time and place and begin to feel those emotions, and rate them on a 1-10 scale. As you feel them begin tapping and repeating the statements. You can really enjoy becoming aware of just *how easy it is to change your emotions*. As with anything, the more you practice this, *the easier and more automatic it becomes*. The more you practice being relaxed in situations that in the past would make you stressed, *the more relaxed you become* in those situations.

Take a moment and imagine all the different times and places it would be useful for you to *take control of your emotions* and *choose the feelings that you want* for yourself. You can achieve this through tapping and letting go of the old emotions, choosing something new and different.

Mind/Body Exercise

1. Label the emotion you want to change and rate it on a scale of one to ten.

2. Begin tapping and state "Even though I feel (label) I still completely and deeply love and accept myself.

3. Cycle through the tapping points and begin to change your statements to "this feeling" and "that feeling".

4. Choose to let the feeling go.

5. Continuing to tap state, "in it's place I choose to feel (new emotion)"

6. Cycle through the points building up this new state.

7. Take a deep breath and check in with yourself. How low on the 1 to 10 scale has that feeling dropped in intensity.

8. Repeat until feeling is completely gone.

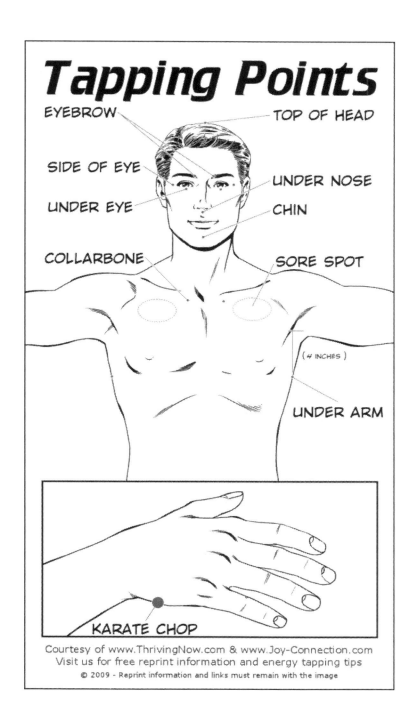

Chapter 9: A Stranger in Your Midst

You are living with a stranger and you have been for quite some time. You know what the stranger looks like and you spend time with him every day. But you really don't know anything about him. You don't know who he is on the inside, or what his real intentions are. Things could be great one minute, and the next the stranger could take everything away from you.

You could kick him out right now and be done with him, or you might get to know what he's like on the inside, and then make up your mind whether he stays or goes.

Getting to Know Your Cigarettes

Imagine one of the cigarettes you smoke throughout the day is right in your hand, where it usually is right before you smoke it. It could be the morning cigarette, or the one at work, or one of the others you used to smoke during your day. As you look at that cigarette, something surprising happens. It begins to grow larger and larger. As it does, you have to set it down because it's just too heavy. As it continues to grow taller, its stands itself up on one end. Before you know it, that cigarette is not only taller than you, but it is at least 30 feet tall, the size of a three- story building!

As you reach out and touch it, the entire cigarette tips over, slamming to the ground. The sheer force cracks it wide open so you can see inside it and even walk the length of it.

Step inside; it's time to explore that cigarette that you have been smoking all this time.

The first thing you might notice is the grayish ash collecting around your feet like the ash from a funeral pyre. Look around and there is no tobacco to be seen. Instead you see a landscape of chemicals and poisons. When you look to your left, you see an old car pumping carbon monoxide into the air. Exhaust fumes are drifting across the landscape.

As you begin to take few steps, the ash gives way to a knee-high pool of acetone – also known as paint stripper. As you wade through, the noxious odor slightly burns the back of your nostrils. The pool of acetone in this cigarette sloshes as you continue your journey. About halfway through this pool you can no longer feel the liquid because your shoes have become chemically dried and cracked.

This cigarette has more in store for you. Just as you make it to the edge of the acetone pool you encounter another unpleasant surprise. As you lift your foot to take a step, you can feel the sticky feeling of tar holding tightly to the soles of your shoes. The acrid stench of fresh tar on a hot summer afternoon reaches your nose now – just as it will from now on every time you take a puff.

As you take step after sticky step, you shuffle into piles of nicotine. You now realize that the old chemical you thought was doing such good things is really a pesticide. Throughout the world nicotine is used to kill insects. As you look down at the nicotine in that cigarette how many dead bugs can you see curled up on the ground?

Suddenly an intense heat pulls your attention to your right. You are greeted with a river of fire as butane burns bright and hot. You can feel the billowing heat as it hits your face, the river of fire making it possible for those cigarettes to burn and create ashy clouds of poison you used to suck into your lungs when you were a smoker.

Even here, this hellish landscape has more ghastly secrets to reveal. In the 1930s and 1940s, one of the greatest atrocities in human history occurred in the Holocaust. Over 6 million Jews, Roma, disabled people, and homosexuals were massacred in Nazi gas chambers. The gas the Nazi's used is found right here in this cigarette you are touring. Each time you smoke you are breathing in the gas used by the Nazis.

Continuing through the cigarette you see piles of arsenic on your left and right. This powder is a heavy metal frequently used as a rat poison. Arsenic is deadly to humans. How much arsenic can your body tolerate? If you were to think through your life, how many piles of arsenic did you force your body to process?

Now we are moving toward the end of the cigarette and the atmosphere is filled with ash, which most closely resembles nuclear fallout, the tons of ash, dirt, and debris a nuclear weapon blasts into the air the atmosphere in the seconds after it explodes. As it falls back to earth, the fallout is coated with deadly radiation. More deaths are caused by radiation poisoning after a bomb explodes than by the initial blast and fire. The acute symptoms of radiation poisoning include blistering, chills, fever, and death. Long term effects include cancer and birth defects. Cigarettes contain radon, a radioactive substance.

The final stop on this tour is the piles of feces and pools of urine at the end of the cigarette. As you see the sludge blocking your way out of the cigarette, you realize that cigarettes release methane, the main component of sewer gas, and contain urea, urine. But you walk through it anyway. After all, you've been putting these things in your mouth for years, so you might as well step into the piles and pools and walk out of the cigarette.

Now look behind you as the cigarette shrinks back to normal size. You watch an old version of you pick it up and smoke it, feeling like you're watching a ridiculous, unrealistic movie. Notice how you feel watching that other you smoke that poisonous, toxic, radioactive, inferno.

In front of you watch a movie of another scenario that used to trigger your smoking. Let the cigarette grow large, as tall as the last one. Now walk through this one seeing all of the same chemicals. Tobacco companies don't make money by actually giving you tobacco. They make cigarettes cheap enough for mass production by filling them up with chemicals.

Feel free to go back and reread this chapter as you walk through this and each subsequent cigarette.

Once you reach the end, watch the old, ridiculous movie of you smoking that cigarette. Once it is over, go through this same process as many times as you need to really understand how evil cigarettes are

So now you know the truth about that stranger you have been living with all of this time. You know now what's inside of this stranger. The stranger has been plotting a terrible crime and waiting for the perfect time. He is planning to steal money from you every week, thousands of dollars a year. He thinks you won't notice. At the same time, he is slowly poisoning you. He wants to kill you and make it look like an accident. He's been doing it to millions of other people as well. You even bought into his lie, and refused to acknowledge that death was waiting at the end of the cigarette.

Now things are different. You are ready to make a new choice, a better decision. You are kicking that stranger out of your home and your life. You are throwing it and all of its stuff out forever. You are lifting the burden and reclaiming your freedom. You know that you deserve to be healthy and happy. Take a deep breath and relax; you've gotten rid of the worst roommate in history.

Chapter 10: Case Study 1

In this chapter and the next we're going to reveal to you one of the techniques we've developed to help clients stop smoking. This is an edited trance-script from a client session. *Feel free* to *sit back and relax as you read*. There is nothing you need to do beyond being curious about just how *you too can change easily.*

Be aware that the first part of the session is a little upsetting, but a brighter future lies in the second half. Remember this is about you reclaiming your freedom so read through this chapter completely before moving onto the next section.

> Hypnotist: "Before we begin just take a moment and consider, aside from you, who else is this change most important to? I know you may think that becoming a non-smoker is only about you, but take a moment and really think about who will benefit most outside of you when you have made this change. It could be anyone, a child, a parent, a lover, a friend.
>
> Client: My mom

Hypnotist: Great. Now just take a few moments to *make yourself comfortable* where you are because one of the easiest ways to go into trance is through the door of comfort and relaxation. You may find that one part of you is more relaxed than the rest. It could be a *pleasant feeling in a hand for a leg*, your breathing, or even inside your mind. Wherever you *find that gentle relaxation* bring your awareness to it and notice what happens. As the saying goes, where your attention goes, energy flows. And I wonder just how your awareness shapes the experience of relaxation.

Client: It increases.

Hypnotist: "That's right, *the relaxation increases*. Did you expect that to happen?

Client: No.

Hypnotist: No, you really didn't and yet there it is. You didn't expect to have that *relaxation deepen* just by you focusing on it and yet it's occurring. Something must be happening on a deeper level. And I wonder just when that process that has already started will continue to *move relaxation throughout your body*.

Client: It's starting

Hypnotist: It is starting, and did you know that this is one of the first signs that you are going into trance now?

Client: No

Hypnotist: Some people think that trance has to look like sleep. What they do not realize is that you go in and out of trances all of the time. Trance is a natural part of your daily rhythm. You can *experience trance right now* whenever you watch a good movie or enjoy a book. When you *go into trance* in this way you keep your eyes open. In fact some of the deepest and most important trances are ones you don't even recognize you're in. So if you want you could keep your eyes open and *enjoy this trance in a new way*.

Now I know *you're here to make an important change*, one that will bring happiness and freedom, and I would like for you to know that *changing is easy*, it's natural. In fact everything changes. The seasons change, fall into winter, into spring, into summer. The tides change, high tide and low tide, the water gently rolling across the sand. The phases of the moon change, full moon, half moon, crescent moon, new moon, a new you. Even at the cellular level at this moment you are changing. Who you were a year ago is not the same as you are today. Over the year your body has let go of old, unhealthy cells and replaced them with new, young, healthy cells, full of life. Even as we speak your body is doing this, which means who you will be an hour from now, day from now, week from now, month from now, and year from now cannot possibly be the same as who you were. And all of that *changing happens easily and automatically*.

One of the many changes you have experienced so far is learning just how powerful your unconscious mind is. And it's important to know that one of the important roles of *your unconscious is to protect you, keep you safe*. Throughout your life it has been doing this. It's what keeps you breathing; it blinks your eyes when something comes too close, it heals you. As we speak *your unconscious mind is keeping you safe* and I wonder in what new and healthy ways can your unconscious protect you and *keep your body healthy and safe*.

You could *imagine yourself in some place comfortable* where you can learn new things and grow as a person. *Imagine standing in front of you is that person who is most important to you, who will be most affected by your decision to stop smoking,* your mom. You can *notice what she is wearing, her posture, the expression on her face.* Maybe you can even hear the sound of her voice. As you take this all in you can begin to *feel the connection you have with her,* the special bond between child and mother. You might remember wonderful memories of her playing with you, teaching you, comforting you, special moments in your life. Take a moment to enjoy *feeling that love that flows from you to her,* to your mom.

Now, as an awareness, drift up and out of your body so you can see both of you. Look now and see you there and your mom over there. And when you are ready, float down and into your mom, *float into the person who cares for you most.* It's like *you can see through her eyes, hear through her ears, and feel how it feels to be her,* to be your mom, *looking back at you,* her child, there. *Begin to feel the love that she,* your mom, has for you, and the special bond between mother and child. Take your time and *enjoy all of those pleasant emotions.*

As her, as your mom, your only job is to watch that you over there go on a journey. Your role is to be in this moment and witness that journey, feeling all of your mom's emotions and experiencing her thoughts.

That you over there has an important choice to make. It's like standing at a fork in the road. To the left is a life filled with cigarettes and smoking and to the right is a full and happy life filled with health and wellbeing.

As mom now, watch your child begin the journey to the left, along the path of cigarettes. What is the first consequence they encounter on the path of smoking?

Client: They smell.

Hypnotist: Take a deep breath and really smell that odor. How does it feel to smell that?

Client: Revolting

Hypnotist: How awful, a mom has to smell something so revolting on her child. Take a moment to really feel that revolting feeling. What consequence is next?

Client: They are coughing, it's hard for them to climb the stairs.

Hypnotist: How does it feel as mom, to watch that?

Client: Very sad.

Hypnotist: It is very sad to realize that your child's health is failing. You have more energy than them. They are coughing and you know how sad it is because of what this means about their health. The coughing is a step down the slippery slope that smoking created. What's the next consequence?

Client: They have to go to the doctor.

Hypnotist: Why?

Client: There's something wrong. They're sick.

Hypnotist: How do you know?

Client: Their color is gone, they can't breathe, and they're in pain.

Hypnotist: Watch and listen in on that doctor's appointment. How do you feel, Mom?

Client: Angry!

Hypnotist: And what is that anger about?

Client: They knew better! They are throwing their life away, stealing my hopes and dreams!

Hypnotist: That's right. Those cigarettes are taking away all of your hopes and dreams for the future. They are stealing your child's health. The cigarettes have tried to control your child. Really be with that anger. It is an appropriate emotion right now.

What does the doctor say?

Client: They have to do tests.

Hypnotist: Watch those tests. All of the needles, stitches, surgeries. What are the results?

Client: Cancer

Hypnotist: Cancer, and as mom hearing your baby has cancer, how do you feel?

Client: Terrified.

Hypnotist: It is terrifying. You don't know what's going to happen, if they'll live or die. You only know that they are about to go through a series of long and painful treatments and there is little you can do to help. You can only be there with your child as those treatments begin. Feel the fear of not knowing if they'll live or die.

What happens next?

Client: They are getting sicker.

Hypnotist: How do you know?

Client: They are coughing up blood.

Hypnotist: What are you feeling in this moment as you see this?

Client: Heart broken.

They are going to die and there's nothing I can do. My baby is in so much pain and will die before me.

Hypnotist: You're right; everything is in the wrong order. Mom is watching her child die. It's enough to tear a heart in half. And all of this was completely avoidable. All of this pain and suffering didn't have to happen.

Go to that moment of death and say good bye to the life you brought into this world and feel that heart break. Feel the pain of burying them, saying your last ever good bye.

Client: It's not fair, it is selfish.

Hypnotist: You're right, it isn't fair that a parent should bury a child, and it's selfish that that child would do something that would take them away from you and leave you behind. Take a moment to be with those feelings.

Now of course you could let those go and allow the feelings to subside. After all, that is only one possibility. They are still at the fork in the road, and because they are here to make such an important change it means your child is *already changing their future and your future* at this very moment. So see them there at that fork in the road ready to take the path to the right, and into a future of new and wonderful possibilities, a future where they get to design the ideal life, where achieving goals just happens naturally and automatically. Maybe you can even see a slight smile on their face as your child begins to run down the path to the right, realizing their future as a non-smoker.

I'm curious: what amazing outcome do they experience first?

Client: They have more energy.

Hypnotist: What lets you know they have more energy?

Client: They are out with friends in the park, having fun.

Hypnotist: And that is an important thing, knowing that they have plenty of energy to be with the people they care about because their body is receiving plenty of oxygen.

How does it feel to see that?

Client: I'm so happy.

Hypnotist: That's right, really feel that happiness. Allow it to fill you from the tips of your toes to the top of your head and back down again. Each time you think about that, the happy feeling grows. You can be happy knowing that because your child took back control, they got to construct the perfect future.

What's the next outcome?

Client: They have more money.

Hypnotist: How do they use it?

Client: They're taking a vacation.

Hypnotist: How do you feel, seeing them on vacation?

Client: Good, they deserve it.

Hypnotist: That's right they really do deserve a vacation, a time to take a break and heal the body and the mind. Really enjoy feeling good as you watch your child having a rest, and being treated with kindness by self and other. Because when there is more energy and more money, who knows what kind of wonderful adventures will be had.

What is the next outcome?

Client: They're healthy.

Hypnotist: And how do you feel knowing that your child is now healthy and living well?

Client: Overjoyed!

Hypnotist: *I wonder how much more joy you can stand to feel seeing the energy, wealth, and health and feeling happy, good,* and even more than that, overjoyed! Pay attention to those feelings that leave you feeling amazing as you watch your child have a longer and happier life. They are achieving every goal they set and even more beyond those goals because *no one can really know just how far a change will go*.

Why not take a moment to congratulate them for having made this lasting change. Let them know just how proud you are of them. You may even want to take some time to share with them some words of wisdom, something that would be wonderful for them to hear.

Now when you are ready, as a consciousness you can drift up and out of Mom so you can see Mom there with you, because it's time to continue the journey in a new way. Float down back into yourself and see mom standing them smiling with pride for everything you have accomplished. Thank her for sharing these moments with you and witnessing your transformation. Give her any special message you would like. You may even want to give her a hug. Pull her into you, allow her to melt into you become a part of who you are again. That's right.

Now in a moment it will be time to come out of trance briefly as you get ready for the next step. You can rest assured knowing that each and every time you go into trance you go deeper and feel even more relaxed. This means that the *changes you are making can sink in on the deepest unconscious level*.

So when you're ready come out of trance just long enough to move on to the next part feeling relaxed, happy, and ready to drift into the next trance.

Take some time now to re-experience this. Here are the steps again:

Choose the person who will be most affected by your decision to QUIT. It could be a child, spouse, lover, parent or friend.

Imagine that person being in front of you. Really see them and notice how they look.

Float up, so you imagine seeing both yourself and the other person below you.

Now float down into them. Feel how that feels. Take a look through their eyes at the "you" over there.

From their perspective, see that the you over there is standing at a fork in the road. The future on the left leads to more cigarettes, the right to a smoke-free and healthy life.

From their perspective, watch that you over there walk down the left-hand path. See everything that awaits you down that path, but from their perspective. Feel how they feel having to watch a loved one experience suffering, and perhaps even death.

Now rewind the movie so that, from the perspective of your loved one, you see yourself walking down the right-hand path. Feel their joy as they watch you experience a new way of being healthy and happy. Notice how everything is different now.

Float out of them, and up, so you can see both them and you below.

Now float back into your own self, and realize that everything has changed.

Chapter 11: Case Study 2

    Hypnotist: Take a moment to recall just *how comfortable the sensation of trance can be.*

As you think about it, I wonder just what comes to mind for you. You could recall the last pleasant trance you had and at what moment you realized you are in a trance. It could be that the trance is starting or perhaps a little further along as you go deeper. Maybe it was toward the end when *you realize something very important and special is taking place.* However you know you are in trance, just be curious about how you know it. Is it the *relaxation of your body*, or the *comfort of your mind* that lets you know first that something is happening, something is changing? Or maybe it's the experience of having thoughts drift by like clouds in a warm afternoon sky. Who's to say just how you know you are going into trance. Only your unconscious can know just when the right moment is to let you know that *trance is happening.*

It is important to take time to go inside for a while because the things that are on the inside can be more important than what's happening on the outside. When you are inside, in comfort and peace, the outside world can carry on doing its own thing. Meanwhile you focus inside yourself and on a deeper level. To the extent that you *find a peace-full place inside*, your body in the outside world can *relax fully*. When you step *inside, change is easy*.

You could allow your thoughts to take you deeper into trance or maybe it's the trance that takes your thoughts to a deeper level. Either way is *easy for you to change*.

Going into hypnosis is a process of learning, and *you are a masterful learner*. In fact you have been learning since the moment you appeared on earth and you will continue to learn for the rest of your life, whether you realize it consciously or not.

Now when you were a small child there were many things you learned. For instance you learned how to read and write. There was a point in your life when you didn't know you didn't know how to read. Then there was a moment when you knew you couldn't read and others could. Finally the big moment came when it is your turn to learn. You go to school and first learn each letter of the alphabet. You start with A, B, C, D, and E all the way through X, Y, and Z. You learn to recognize the shape of each letter and its name. You practice writing each letter, one at time. Maybe at some points it's a little tricky. It's easy to confuse a b with a d when you're small. You do learn with some practice and you continue to move on.

You next learn that letters have short sounds and long sounds. You discover that some are consonants and some are vowels. Eventually, when the time is right you put the letters together to make sounds and those sounds turn into words. Some words are small and some are big. With a little practice and sounding out those new words your abilities grow.

Eventually those words turn into whole sentences and those sentences transform into entire stories that you are reading with ease. In fact, you don't even have to think about it, it's just automatic. I wonder what new and amazing things you are learning right at this moment and will continue to learn.

Now I'd like you to imagine that you are sitting in a comfortable movie theater. And in a moment a movie will begin to play on that screen in front of you. That movie is going to be a special feature. You will have the opportunity now to watch the experience of smoking your first cigarette. So you'll be able to see yourself on the screen, seeing where you were then, as well as anyone else who was there with you. As you do this, pay careful attention to your reaction with that first puff.

That movie can begin now. It will play from the beginning of that first cigarette all the way through to when you are finished. Notice the expression on your face, listen for the cough, and be aware of your reaction to that cigarette.

Once that film has ended I would like for you to *drain all of the color out of the final moment of the movie*, so it becomes black and white. Now that black-and-white movie is going to *play backwards this time at twice the speed*. It will start at the end and go all the way to the beginning. It's like you pushed rewind on the DVD player. Do that one more time, but this time play that black-and-white movie backwards at four times the speed, so that the people in it, the cigarette, are all moving backwards, and are hard to make out.

In a moment, the movie will begin to play forward again, this time from the beginning to the end, but it will move at three times its old speed. It's like you have pushed the fast-forward button on your DVD player.

This time, *darken the movie*; the *image becomes dim and dark*. Watch that dim, defocused, and black and white movie play backwards at four times the speed.

This wouldn't be a movie without a soundtrack, so add in some music and sound effects that are funny and ridiculous. Many people like to add circus music, or perhaps you have some other sounds that make you want to laugh. With that new soundtrack in place, watch that film play at five times the speed from the beginning all the way to the end. You may notice how ridiculous it now seems.

Finally, you can take that old movie and *push it way off into the distance*, so it gets smaller, and smaller. You can take it out so far that you can no longer see it. It is gone.

Now it is time to do something different. You can watch many different types of movies in this theater. Why not begin choosing movies that move you toward your goal? To help you choose the right movie, you can invite in a very special guest. I'd like for you to ask a much younger you to join you. This younger version of you can be about six or seven years old. He or she can come in and sit right next to you, because the two of you are about to share a special experience.

That younger you is at an age where they can learn many life lessons. You can *teach the younger you skills or wisdom* that they may need that will make all the difference for them growing up.

You may want to begin by teaching that little you some special skills. For example, you already know how to use EFT and the backward spin. How powerful will it be for that child of six or seven to be able to use these tools as they grow up? I wonder what kind of difference it will make as they grow through the teen years to where you are today. Take a moment and teach the younger you any skills that will make all the difference for them as they grow up, and for you now.

One more thing that you really ought to teach that younger you is the ability to say "no", or maybe even, "Hell No!" That child may have learned that it's not polite to say no, but now they can learn that there are *times and places where it is important to be able to say no* in an assertive way. In fact that younger you can really rebel at the right time, whenever they have the opportunity to say "no" when it's right for them.

There may be other things that that younger you really needs to know, that will *change everything for them in a positive way*. Whatever those things are, it may take some time to teach them. You could also share with that little you sitting there any words of wisdom or comfort that you have to offer. If you could tell your younger self anything that would help them become more resourceful, healthier, and happier, what would you say? Share that with them now.

Because that much younger you has now learned these skills, they will be available when he or she, or you, needs them, especially when offered that first cigarette.

In a moment a new movie is going to begin to play. This new movie is going to be about a *skilled and resourceful you, saying no to the offer of the first cigarette.* In fact this movie will show you exactly how good it is to be a non-smoker because it will continue beyond that offered cigarette and show you your whole life up to this moment. Your only job is to watch and *feel good see yourself being assertive, in control, smoke-free* and acting for your true self-interest.

So the two of you, you and the younger you, can watch that you on-screen acting differently using the skills you've taught. Watch them say no to that offer of that first cigarette, and feeling good standing up for your own well-being. After that moment there will be another time when maybe someone else offers a cigarette and you get to feel even better watching yourself say no again. As time goes by there may be another instance when someone offers you a cigarette and you have the opportunity to *feel good saying* NO! Go through every instance of saying no and feel good watching that movie, showing you going from where you were up to your present age, everything in this new movie is different. You are creating a healthy life with the flexibility to say "No" whenever the time is right.

Once the movie has ended, take a moment to thank that younger, 6- or 7-year-old you, and give them any final pieces of wisdom that they may need in order to feel good, being a non-smoker. When you are finished, something amazing happens. The younger you gets up and walks over to the screen. As if by magic, he or she literally steps into the screen and becomes the age you were when you said "no" to that first cigarette. Now watch as that new movie plays again, watching the younger you say "NO!" and feel even better, knowing you have helped *change the past.* Remembering that each time you say "no" to a cigarette your good feelings grow. Take every opportunity to *say no and feel good.* That movie plays through until the you on the screen is the same age as you are now in the theater.

Now it's your turn to experience this from the inside out. You've had fun watching yourself on the screen do amazing things, and now you get to really *feel how good it feels to say "no" to cigarettes for yourself.* So walk up to that screen and step inside, becoming the age you were when you were first offered cigarettes. Feel how good it really feels to *say "no" and enjoy that feeling.* Enjoy standing up for you and for the things you want in life. Because as you go beyond that cigarette, to each and every other opportunity you have to *say "no", your good feelings continue to grow.* As the days, weeks, months and years pass, and *you're living smoke free.* You are the person you want to be. *You are in control of all of your choices.* Eventually that movie reaches the point where you are your current age, feeling good, knowing on a deep level that something has indeed changed.

Only as quickly as *you can keep these learnings*, and feel good, begin the process of reorienting completely to the outside world, feeling refreshed, awake, alert and simply fantastic.

You can *allow all of the positive changes to continue on the deepest unconscious level*, so that even at night as you sleep and dream, your neurology rewires itself. *Your brain selects the healthiest, most resourceful behaviors for you*, so that your life becomes more of what you wish for it to be.

Now that you have read through this session, you can re-experience it for yourself. Here are the steps:

Mind Exercise

1. Find yourself in a movie theater. A movie plays of you smoking your first cigarette. Watch it to the end, noticing how bad it tasted then, perhaps watching the younger you coughing and vomiting. Freeze it at the last frame.

2. Now begin to change aspects of the movie. Make it black and white first. Now run it backwards at twice the speed, then backwards at four times the speed, then forwards at three times the speed. This begins to scramble the memory in your mind.

3. Now you can add circus music, make the movie small and dark, and finally push it into the distance, so it is virtually invisible.

4. Now invite a much younger you only 6 or 7 years old, to join you in the theater, even younger than the you in the movie, and teach this younger you all the skills you have learned, especially the skills you have already learned in this book. Teach them EFT and the backward spin for example.

5. Because you have taught this much younger you these skills, these skills have also been learned by the you in the movie. Play the movie again, with both you and the much younger you watching. This time it's different; the you in the movie says "no" to that first cigarette.

6. Allow the movie to play on; the you in the movie saying "no" whenever a cigarette or something else harmful is offered.

7. Now the much younger you says goodbye to you and floats into the movie, magically becoming the age when the first cigarette was offered and getting to experience saying "no" to all those cigarettes.

8. You can float into the movie and experience saying "no" until you reach your current age, and return to the complete and integrated you in the here and now.

Chapter 12: Escaping from Tigers

In ancient times humans faced many dangers in the natural world. There were all sorts of animals that were out hunting for an easy meal. Some animals were small while others were ferocious and stealthy. Blood-thirsty animals are brutal. They don't care whom they hurt and they are only interested in the bottom line. What matters to them is how they will prosper. They don't think twice about the cost of their greed to others.

However, we humans are intelligent, and we have devised ways to elude predators. We learned a long time ago that the closer something deadly comes toward us, the more in danger we are. This in turn means that the closer something deadly comes, the more the amygdala, the part of your brain responsible for the "Fight or Flight" response becomes active and the stronger the instinct is to get away, to escape from danger. If you are out in the jungle and you caught the eye of a tiger, your survival instincts will kick in. You will move as quickly as possible to a safe location where the tiger cannot get you. With each step the tiger takes toward you, you match it with a step in the other direction, keeping your distance from danger.

Once the tiger loses interest, once it is clear that it will not be getting an easy meal from you, it backs away. With each step the tiger takes away from you, the more relaxed and safe you can feel. The further away that tiger goes, the easier your life becomes.

No sane person would offer themselves up for the tiger as a free meal. Doing so would go against hundreds of thousands of years of evolution. We do things that are in our best interest, but sometimes people need a reminder of what the tiger is and where it's hiding. When you know where the tiger is, you know its secret haunts and you can avoid them.

My question to you is, will you lie down and be eaten by the tiger, or will you make a swift escape?

The first step to escaping is by holding a cigarette the way you would have in the past, as if you were going to smoke it. As you hold that cigarette begin to think about the cost of it. I don't mean cost in a monetary sense; I'm speaking of the true price you and those around you pay because of that little thing. You can consider how *that cigarette steals money from you.* Recall how much money you've wasted each week on that nasty thing. You can also recall how much more expensive your healthcare might be, because smoking is a risky behavior. You could even project your mind to the future and carefully consider how much money you will burn up in healthcare costs. People who face smoking-related health care expenses can end up millions of dollars in debt because of medical bills. I'm not asking you here to give any, "Yes, but it won't be me" answers. I'm asking you to *get in touch with righteous anger and disgust, and to attach those feelings to cigarettes.* Just imagine how it would feel to be millions of dollars in debt, unable to pay them back because you are still sick. And the worst part is that this was all preventable.

I often ask my clients how much they enjoy burning money. They immediately respond that they do not. However, this is exactly what you're doing when you smoke. There is no difference between spending money on cigarettes or smoking-related health costs and going outside, dumping all of your savings into a trashcan, pouring lighter fluid on it, and taking a match to it. How does it feel to stand there and watch your money burn?

How does it feel to imagine that? Take a moment to get in touch with those feelings. The more *you can feel the anger, sadness, or fear while holding that tiger in your fingers* the better.

As you begin to *lift the cigarette slowly toward your mouth, feel those bad emotions building*. Carefully think about all of those things cigarettes are stealing from you. With *each movement toward your face, those bad feelings can double*. In fact you may find it *reach the point that you do not want to lift that cigarette any closer*. After all why would you want to bring a hungry tiger close to your face? It is just waiting for the opportunity to maul you.

If you don't find it difficult to bring that cigarette toward your face, then *stop* and take a moment to *build those bad feelings* again. Perhaps you will *recall all of the awful things about that cigarette as you try to bring it closer*. You can *remember the bleach, arsenic, lighter fluid, and industrial cleaner contained in that cigarette as it moves a little closer*. Or maybe you will choose to *call to mind the methane and urea added to your smokes as the cigarette moves closer*. Both of these substances are found you human urine and feces. How would it *feel bringing something soaked in human waste to your lips and then place it in your mouth*?

When *you can no longer bring the cigarette to your lips*, and you *feel like you want to throw that cigarette away*, it's time to start building good feelings. So as you slowly begin to *move the cigarette away from you, recall all of the wonderful things you will get from being a non-smoker*. You can *think about all the reasons you are quitting as it moves away*. Bring to mind how good it feels to know that your body is already healing itself. You are already beginning the process of *healing your lungs, healing your heart, and healing other vital organs as it continues to move away*. How are you being as a person when you are like this? You may find that the further you *move that cigarette away from your mouth, the more those good feelings build*. As that *cigarette moves away you are increasing your health, improving your relationships, and expanding your bank account*. With each *movement of that cigarette away from your face you are extending your life*. Think of how many more minutes you will have added to your life because you have made this choice now.

Enjoy this process and take your time to fully feel the good emotions that come from letting go of something that had been choking you in the past. Once your hand has completely lowered, begin the process again. *Raise the cigarette slowly as you feel the disgust, sadness, worry, fear, anger* and any other negative feelings you have tied to the cigarette. Once you *feel completely repulsed with the cigarette*, begin to lower it again, recalling all of the good feelings that come from letting go of this old habit. Take your time to *build the happiness, joy, energy, freedom, and everything else as the cigarette is pushed away* and *you know that you have accomplished this change*.

Repeat this process until you find yourself no longer wanting to lift cigarette at all. This may take several repetitions. With this process you are training your brain to respond in the opposite way of how it used to when holding cigarettes. You're teaching yourself to recognize the tiger in the jungle. If that tiger moves closer, your natural instinct is to move away. When the tiger moves away your automatic response is to feel good.

Remember, the key to success with this exercise is to *really build up those negative feelings as you move the cigarette closer*, and to *build up those positive feelings when that cigarette moves away*. It is the feelings that drive the change, and the more you can *feel anger, disgust and fear as the cigarette approaches*, and *feel relief, freedom and joy as the cigarette moves away* the better the exercise works! The stronger you make these feelings and the more deeply you recognize them, the more completely the learning will sink in.

You will notice that once you have conditioned the response you may even *find that just lifting a cigarette makes you feeling awful*, while putting it down creates amazingly good feelings automatically. When you condition this response with repetition, it will automatically happen and you can *feel relaxed knowing that your brain is rewiring itself in new and productive ways*.

Mind- Body Exercise

1. Hold cigarette in the hand with which you used to smoke.

2. Get in touch with all of the negative feelings you have about that cigarette. You can imagine all of the things that cigarette stole from you and anything else negative that is linked to that habit.

3. Only lift that cigarette as slowly as you can really feel those horrible emotions. You must be feeling the emotions as you do this. Lift it until you no longer want to or can't anymore.

4. As you bring the cigarette down feel the relief and everything positive that comes with successfully kicking the habit. Spend time building these good feelings.

5. Repeat until *you can longer lift the cigarette.* You either physically can't lift the cigarette or *find it too disgusting.*

Chapter 13: 6 Steps to Freedom

One of the fears that many of my clients have when they first book their session is that once they give up smoking they're going to start gaining weight. Many of them believe that the weight gain is due to some change in their body chemistry.

While they are not wrong that some people have experienced weight gain, the reasons are not what they suspect. Something like this occurs when a person goes through a process called symptom substitution. This means that the underlying need behind smoking hasn't been met, so the brain just finds another way of meeting that need that is equally unhealthy. My clients discover very quickly that it doesn't have to be that way.

You, on the other hand, will have a very different experience because of the technique you are about to learn. The technique presented in this chapter is designed to eliminate any possibility of negative symptom substitution. In fact, it turns the process of symptom substitution to your benefit. This means that you get all of the benefit of being a non-smoker as well as having that underlying need met in a healthy and resourceful way.

Now before we get into the actual process, there are a couple of beliefs that will be helpful for you to hold. The first is that there is a positive intention behind very behavior. This does not mean that every behavior is good or useful, but that the underlying drive for the behavior is positive. The part of you responsible for the smoking wanted something good for you. It may be something like feeling more relaxed, or having more breaks. Those desires are good in and of themselves, even though the behavior (smoking) is not. It's only a matter of redirecting the energy so that you can have that need met and do so in a new way that is more ecological to you as a whole person throughout your life.

Think of it this way: you are a very intelligent person. It's true; you wouldn't have made it to this point in your life if you weren't intelligent on both the conscious and unconscious levels. This automatically means that your actions are driven by intelligent and good motivations. But sometimes misunderstandings distort those intentions into unresourceful or even self-destructive behaviors.

You might consciously know what the positive intention is behind your smoking, or you might not. For our purposes it doesn't really matter. The result will be the same as you replace smoking with a positive life-affirming behavior.

The second helpful belief is that you have every resource you need. This means that inside of you, you have all of the skills and abilities needed in order to create change. You should believe this because it is true. Throughout your life you have been constantly acquiring new knowledge, skills, beliefs, and values. All of these things can be pieced together in new and wonderful ways that create and change behaviors. On an evolutionary level you come from a long tradition of success. All of your ancient ancestors were immensely resourceful and successful; you wouldn't be on the Earth if they were not. This means that you also carry this same level of resourcefulness inside of you.

As we go on, hold on to these two beliefs: *every behavior has a positive intention*, and *you have all the resources you need*. They will make the process of change natural and easy. Understanding these two ideas on a deep level will help with the next steps, not only to create change but also to increase your respect for the deeper parts of your mind that are constantly working for your well-being, happiness, and success.

The technique presented in this chapter is all about re-routing the neural networks connected with smoking to a new and more positive direction. An easy way to think about the smoking problem is that it consists of a series of neural connections inside your brain. There are neurons connected to the trigger, neurons that allow you to have good and bad feelings associated with smoking, neurons connected to thoughts about the cigarettes, neurons relating to the taste and feeling of the cigarette, and so on. When making this change it is important to give a new purpose to each of those neurons and neural networks by making new connections.

Neural networks that are no longer in use go through a process of neural pruning. This means that they are either transformed, or they die off. Evolution says, and neuroscience confirms, that these neural networks are going to fight for survival. This means if you do not find a new purpose for the neural network connected to cigarettes, they are going to try to find ways to keep the habit going.

With this technique you will be working on two levels; the first level is all about finding the positive intention behind the smoking, and the second is to create new ways of meeting that positive intention. This meets the emotional needs that in the past drove you to smoke. On the neurological level this works by finding ways to allow those neurons to continue doing what they've been doing, but now acting in ways that are far more beneficial. This means that your emotional needs are met, and the neural networks become your allies in changing your behavior.

People who quit, and then end up picking up another bad habit, do so because they haven't met these two needs. This type of change isn't only about the nicotine, as that is out of your system within a few days. It is also about negotiating between your emotions and your neurology.

This process consists of six simple steps. If you take the time to sit down and focus on it, you will most likely see results the first time through. You won't need to come back to this again once the change has happened. You can also use this process for any other type of behavior that you would like to change. It is a versatile technique and one of my favorites.

In the following section I will break down the steps simply, so that you can do this on your own and see immediate and lasting results. We suggest doing this process either as a closed-eyes experience, or by using a pendulum to communicate with the unconscious mind. I will cue you when to close your eyes and immerse yourself in the experience.

Step One- Recognize the Problem

(this can be eyes open or closed. This step is necessary for either the closed-eye or the pendulum method.)

This step is very straightforward. Take time to call to mind smoking and that old part that used to want the cigarettes. This is the part of you that used to reach for the cigarettes or remind you it was time to smoke. Bring to mind the respect for this part as it was doing something for you in the past. Now you know you can do things differently. What you're actually doing here is activating the neural network inside of your brain connected with smoking. This is where the change will be made.

Step Two- Establish Unconscious Communication

Did you know you could communicate with your unconscious mind? In fact the techniques we have been using throughout this book are ways in which you've been able to establish communication back and forth with your unconscious in an indirect way. You have done this through the words used in the book as well as the images, feelings, and words we have invited you to generate for yourself.

Up to this point it has been indirect communication, because you have not been actively speaking to the part of you responsible for smoking and listening for responses. This time, in this process, we are going to do just that. You're actually going to be able to have the conversation with your unconscious mind that will change feelings and re-purpose those neural connections.

Now there are many ways to do this, but I'm going to suggest that you use one of the two ways I explain here. This is simply because we do not have the luxury of doing this process face-to-face.

The first approach is to have a deep awareness of your sensory experience. In a moment I will ask you to close your eyes. While doing this, take a moment to thank yourself for everything your unconscious mind does for you. Your unconscious mind is always there monitoring your heart rate and breathing. Your unconscious is the part of **you** that allows learning to happen, and it's the part of you that dreams at night. In fact your body is an extension of your unconscious mind. I wonder in what ways you can say thank you to your unconscious for taking care of your physical well-being. (Close your eyes and do this part now, then open your eyes and continue reading.)

In a moment I am going to ask you to close your eyes again and and this time as you thank your unconscious mind, notice the feelings and emotions that you feel inside your body. This is unconscious communication. You can't consciously decide to experience a specific emotion at any time because emotions are within the control of your unconscious mind. In order to feel the emotion of your choice, you would have to take some steps in between thinking, "I'm going to feel happy today," and actually feeling that way. For some people that may mean thinking about the good things to come, for others it may be remembering happy memories. Or perhaps for you it's something completely different. Regardless, you will have to communicate with the unconscious mind to develop those emotions. So now, as you're feeling whatever good sensation may be developing from thanking your unconscious mind, you can comfortably consider this as a type of communication between your conscious mind and your unconscious mind. (Close your eyes and do this part now, then open your eyes and continue reading.)

Now take a step further and ask your unconscious mind for a "yes" signal. You may need to repeat "yes" a few times in your mind before you notice the response. The response could be a feeling, twitching finger, or maybe an image in your mind. Another way to get a "yes" is to stand up and notice your balance point, and then think, "Yes…yes…yes" and notice which way your body tends to lean (for most people, the body leans forward for "yes"). Now think, "No…no…no". You will likely notice your body leaning in the opposite direction! The important thing here is that the signal, whatever it may be, is distinct and replicable.

Once you have that signal, *thank you unconscious mind once again*. The process presented in this chapter is really about gratitude. You should take every opportunity to *thank your unconscious mind throughout this process*. It really is amazing how far such overt gratitude can take you in creating this change. Aside from that, it also feels good! (Close your eyes and do this part now)

Now that you have a yes, it's time to establish a "no" signal. Ask your unconscious mind for that "no" signal and be clear that you mean NO and not KNOW. Spell it out for your unconscious mind, N-O. Repeat this process until you notice the, "no" signal. Once you have the "no" remember to thank your unconscious for communicating with you in this way. (Close your eyes and do this part now)

Alternative Method: The Pendulum

Some people may not be used to noticing their emotions and feelings Therefore there is another strategy you can use to establish unconscious communication. It's based on the principle of "ideomotor" movement. This is a type of movement in the muscles that occurs below conscious awareness, and is characterized by tiny, sometimes imperceptible, twitches in the muscles such as the fingers. These types of movements can be invisible to the naked eye. This means we're going to use a tool, a pendulum, help us to amplify the responses so you can detect them.

This strategy is sometimes referred to as the pendulum method. While some people may believe that this is weird or strange, it actually is a natural physiological response that has been tested and shown to be scientifically valid. To do this you need a pendulum. This could be anything from a charm hanging on a necklace, to a paper clip attached to a piece of string. Some people like to have special pendulum for this type of work, although that is not necessary. All you need is something with a little weight hanging on a string, thread or chain.

Utilizing unconscious movement has long been a part of hypnotherapy and has been studied by the scientific community since the nineteenth century. The most basic example of this is having a participant hold the pendulum and simply will it to swing clockwise or counterclockwise. Participants sit and think to themselves over and over again, "clockwise, clockwise," while making pictures in their minds of the pendulum swinging that way. To their surprise, the pendulum begins to swing in that direction. This is because the muscles in the fingers are unconsciously responding to the command communicated by the thought.

You will be using this same principle to establish unconscious communication. To do this sit somewhere comfortable with the pendulum. It's ideal to have a flat surface on which you can rest your elbow while using the pendulum. Place the chain with the string between your thumb and either your index finger or your middle finger. Either way is fine.

Just as in the previous approach, we will establish unconscious communication by asking for a test signal. Hold the pendulum still and ask your unconscious mind for a "yes". Think, "Yes…yes…yes…" Repeat this until you see a clear swing for yes. This may be in a circle going clockwise or counterclockwise, or it may swing in a straight line either left to right or front to back. Remember to thank your unconscious mind once you have that signal.

Do the same to acquire the "no" signal. The "yes" and the "no" will have distinctly different swings, often in an opposite sense. For example, the "yes" signal might be a clockwise rotation, while the "no" is counter-clockwise. Or a "yes" signal might be forward-backward, in a straight line, while the "no" signal is side-to side. You will be able to differentiate between the two easily. You can go back and retest, asking for the "yes" and "no" again until you're sure and you will be pleasantly surprised to find the "yes" and "no" signals are the same as the first time. Remember that each time you ask something from your unconscious mind, it is important to thank it. Not only does this gratitude feel good, but it also creates motivation and further response potential.

Step Three - Finding the Positive Intention

As we showed at the beginning of this chapter, there is a positive intention behind every behavior, even smoking. You may consciously know what it is or not. You may even think you know consciously, while your unconscious mind knows the truth. It's important to establish what the positive intention is, so that your unconscious mind can begin to generate new ways of accomplishing the intention. But it is not important whether your unconscious mind lets you consciously know just what the positive intention is.

Begin by asking your unconscious mind if it's willing to help you make this change. Wait a few moments for the yes signal to appear. Then thank your unconscious mind. (Close your eyes and do this part now or use your pendulum.)

If you should get a "no" signal, ask again. If you get a "no" signal once more, ask one more time to be sure. If you get a third "no," you'll need to take a step back and negotiate with yourself. Perhaps now is not the right time for this change. You might, however, only need to approach it from a different angle. You can begin by asking the unconscious mind if it's willing to change just one small part of the problem. This could be the time you smoke or the number of cigarettes you smoke each day. The idea is to try to get the unconscious mind to agree to make one small change in the direction of your becoming smoke-free. Once your unconscious mind is on board, and gets comfortable with the idea of change, it will be prepared to make bigger changes. This type of issue (a persistent "no" signal) is extremely rare. It is far more common for you to get a "yes" signal quickly and easily.

Do not move onto the next step until you have the "yes."

Next ask your unconscious mind to find the positive intention, or intentions, behind smoking, and to give you a "yes" signal once that intention is found, even though you may not know what this is consciously . This may take a few moments, but you will begin to feel either "yes", or see the pendulum swing in the right direction. Again thank your unconscious. (Close your eyes and do this part now, or use your pendulum.)

You can now ask if the unconscious is willing to share that positive intention with you. You may get a "yes" or a "no." Either way is fine. You don't need to know the positive intention consciously. But remember to thank your unconscious mind either way. Each time you thank it, *allow that feeling of gratitude to grow.* (Close your eyes and do this part now, or use your pendulum.)

Step Four - Generate New Behaviors

The next step is to begin to find new ways of realizing the positive intention. Think of this as a re-purpose of the neural network associated with smoking. The intention is still there, but the behavior changes and becomes useful.

At this point it is not useful for your conscious mind to be involved. In fact it is better that it remain uninvolved. After all, you've already spent a long time trying to consciously change this behavior, with little luck. It's time to *allow your unconscious mind to take charge of the change* for you. So ask your unconscious mind to generate 37 new and resourceful ways of meeting this intention, and to give you a "yes" signal when it has done so. (Close your eyes and do this part now, or use your pendulum.)

Once you have the "yes", thank your unconscious mind again. (Close your eyes and do this part now, or use your pendulum.)

You may find that some of the ideas come to your conscious awareness, and that is perfectly fine. Just know that underneath the surface there are significantly more possibilities being generated.

Step Five - Narrow the Choices

Of course having 37 options available at the unconscious level may not be particularly useful, unless the unconscious chooses one to actually implement! So now it's time to begin narrowing down the choices and to get the conscious mind involved.

Ask the unconscious mind to narrow the choices down to the three most resourceful and healthy ways to meet that positive intention and allow you to quit smoking for life. Ask your unconscious mind to give you a "yes" signal when it has done so. Remember to thank the unconscious mind when you get the "yes." (Close your eyes and do this part now, or use your pendulum.)

Now ask your unconscious to choose the new behavior that best suits you as a complete person and is ecological for your relationships while still meeting that positive intention. Wait again for the "yes" signal. When you get it, your unconscious mind may let your conscious mind know what that new behavior is, but if doesn't, that's fine too. It may be something that you expected or it could be something completely new and different. Enjoy being pleasantly surprised by just how resourceful you can be at solving problems and achieving your goals when you act as a complete person. (Close your eyes and do this part now, or use your pendulum.)

Take a few moments to really feel a deep sense of gratitude for the deeper part of you that has found this solution. Feel good in knowing that there are parts of you that are much wiser than you could possibly consciously suspect. (Close your eyes and do this part now, or use your pendulum.)

Step Six - Final Check

Ask your unconscious mind to go through your experiences, personality, goals, and relationships, and make sure that this new behavior is congruent with all of the different aspects of your life. By this I mean evaluating the degree to which the new behavior will seamlessly mesh with your lifestyle and relationships. If there is a conflict, that's no problem. Simply go back to the last step and ask the unconscious mind to select another behavior. (Close your eyes and do this part now, or use your pendulum.)

Once the right behavior has been selected, and you have checked it for congruence, ask your unconscious mind to put that behavior into place for a trial period. Give yourself a timeframe in which to test it, to be sure that it's the right one for you. Oftentimes people choose a test period of about two weeks. This gives just enough time to become comfortable with the new behavior, and to test it in a number of different contexts to be sure it is right for you. (Close your eyes and do this part now or use your pendulum)

Once you've done this, take a moment to imagine yourself later today, tomorrow, and next week using this new behavior and enjoying being completely smoke-free. You know how good it is to succeed at this. Step into the emotions and build up the movie in your mind with is much detail as possible. Think of this as watching a movie of your future, with all of the changes in place. The more detailed, bright, big, and close you can make this movie, the better you can feel.

See yourself in a number of different times and places where you would previously have smoked but now are doing something differently, then step into the movie and experience it from the inside. (Close your eyes and do this part now.)

Congratulate yourself and your unconscious, and thank yourself for everything you've done both consciously and unconsciously to help create this change on a deep level. (Close your eyes and do this part now.)

Mind Exercise

1. Decide whether you will use the pendulum method, or rely on the sensations your unconscious mind creates

2. Call to mind the problem of smoking and the different instances in which you smoked.

3. As your unconscious mind if it is willing to help change this and wait for the yes signal (from the pendulum, or a feeling).

4. Remember to thank your unconscious mind every time you receive a response.

5. Ask your unconscious mind to let you know when it has found the positive intention behind the smoking behavior.

6. Ask your unconscious to generate 37 healthy new ways of satisfying that intention and to signal yes when it has done so.

7. Instruct your unconscious to select one and to signal yes.

8. Have your unconscious check that this new behavior fits in with who you are as a person, your relationships, and your overall life.

9. If your unconscious mind signals no then ask it to select a different behavior. If it signals yes then thank that deeper part of you.

10. Practice the new behavior in your imagination before ending the session.

Chapter 14: Changing Your Life

I'd like to start this chapter by congratulating you. You have successfully worked your way through the major steps needed to change your life. At this point only a few small pieces remain to be put into place.

Testing

Some people, who make it to the point of being completely done with cigarettes, still find themselves wanting to test the process. Such people are motivated by a disbelief that *you can change as quickly as you have*. These people think, "Maybe I should go out and smoke a cigarette just to be sure." I'm sure that I don't like chewing tobacco, so I don't need to go out and test that. I'm also sure that when I was little I enjoyed very sweet treats but as an adult I don't, and I do not and have no need to test that. I know that when I was little I liked the things children like, but as an adult my palate has become far more refined. I don't have the desire to go and test if that's for real.

Because you have actually made it to this point, it is clear that *change can happen quickly and efficiently*. You may be thinking, "Well I'd better be sure." Perhaps you believe that you have to expose yourself to the *cigarettes you don't like now* in order to know that *you do not like cigarettes*. Those beliefs are not only counterproductive, they are simply wrong. Why would you partake in something knowing that *you will not enjoy smoking anymore*? It's far more useful to spend your time knowing that there are things in life that you definitely enjoy and pursuing those things. It's no longer necessary to take part in things that you are certain will bring you damage and harm.

To put this simply, don't go looking for problems where there are none. Enjoy the fact that *you have indeed changed* and you are now making decisions that are in your best interest. It is far more useful to spend your time being serious about all of the ways in which *you can fully improve your health and your life*.

Where your attention goes your energy flows. If you spend all your time thinking about the "what-if's," you give them a second chance at coming true. But when you spend your time being curious about all the possibilities that await you, *your energy will move you toward these possibilities and bring you future happiness*.

Understanding Your Identity

As I said at the beginning of this book, *you are not a smoker*, you never have been, and you never will be. I am currently typing these words out on my computer; does that mean I am a typist? Most certainly not. I know that I am much more than any particular activity I participate in at any given time. I am not defined by my activities and neither are you. Identity is flexible, unlimited, and is defined by you alone.

Sure, other people have their own ideas about who you are. They may even think that they understand you completely and fully from the inside out. You know that cannot be possibly true, because you are much more than any frame that anyone else tries to put around you. Your identity stretches beyond being a child, sibling, parent, worker, and most especially "smoker." Whatever labels someone else gives you, understand that you are more than that. What is amazing is that *you are actually much more even than the identities you give yourself.* Please take the time to appreciate the positive possibilities before you, and resist reducing their number by believing in a fixed definition of who you are and what you can do.

As you consider these ideas, I wonder what they can tell you about who you are as a complete person. According to my friend John Overdurf, all hypnosis is self-hypnosis, and the most powerful hypnotic events are the stories we tell ourselves and the stories we tell others about ourselves. Every time you tell someone else about who you are, you are strengthening the "personal identity narratives" you have inside your head. Each and every time you tell yourself stories about yourself, you're strengthening those narratives as well. The great news is that you get to decide which stories to pay attention to and share with others, and which ones are no longer accurate or useful.

With all of these things in mind, I would like you to consider that even if you were to smoke a cigarette at some point in the future, that act would not make you a smoker. This is essential for you to understand on a deep level. If I have a cigarette as I'm typing this, I still know on a deep level that ultimately I am not a smoker. In fact I have smoked in the past, but I made the decision that it was not right for me. Even when I smoked, I knew that I was not smoker. The only thing that would make me a smoker would be deciding to identify with being a smoker.

You may previously have chosen to identify yourself as a smoker. However you may find that that it is more useful for you to *identify yourself as an ex-smoker, a non-smoker, someone who is smoke free*, and someone who is free of smoking. Think of it this way: if a non-smoker has one puff of a cigarette and then puts it out, does that act make them a smoker? Of course not. So what about a smoker who puffs on a cigarette and then puts it out? Different people can do the same thing and yet one may think of themselves as a smoker and the other does not. The only difference between the two individuals is how they choose to identify themselves. The person who chooses to identify as a non-smoker knows that they could have one cigarette, find it absolutely revolting, and then go on with the rest of their day knowing they are smoke-free.

On the other hand, if you think you're a smoker and you take a drag from a cigarette, find it disgusting, and put it out, you allow your mind to attach to the act. This attachment leads to constructing the hallucinated identity that "I am a smoker again." *Put that out* of your mind, *it's* a *disgusting* thought.

At the end of the day, everyone's identity is subjective, a result of the functions of the mind, physiology, culture, and memories. Your identity is a function of where you choose to place your awareness. If you decide right now that *you are a non-smoker*, and you put an emotional energy behind it, you will find that your physiology, your thoughts, as well as the people around you, will act differently.

So what story are you going to tell yourself about your identity? What story will you tell others? Those who tell themselves and others that they are smokers, or even ex-smokers, usually end up being smokers. Which is to say, they end up being a slave to the cigarette companies.

Those who *choose to identify as being smoke-free or a non-smoker* generate the emotional energy needed in order for them to truly enjoy what it is like to be a non-smoker.

Recovery Strategies

Many people see very quick results going through the processes described in this book. In fact, more often than not, they throw out their cigarettes and lighters before they actually reach the end of the program. These people feel the emotions necessary to be smoke-free. They know the satisfaction of freedom and health of being smoke-free, as well as the disgust, anger and fear associated with cigarettes. They fully and completely experience the power of the human mind. The people who are most successful in this process are those who can commit themselves wholeheartedly and persistently.

Resiliency lies at the core of any real change we make in our lives. This means that whenever we catch ourselves thinking in a way that is less than resourceful, we give ourselves the space to "reset," and then to resume making progress toward our goal.

The key to success is to remember that we always have the option to transform failure into feedback. When Thomas Edison created the world's first light bulb, he didn't get it on the first try. In fact it took him over 1,000 attempts before he found a filament that would last for more than a few hours. When asked how he felt about failing a thousand times, he had an interesting answer. He said that he had not failed, but had instead succeeded in discovering a thousand ways a light bulb cannot be made!

If your experience hasn't matched your expectation, this doesn't mean it's not *a chance to learn and grow*. It simply means you have the opportunity to try something different. So stick with it. Throughout this process you are literally re-training your neurology, rewiring your brain. The more often you practice and the more frequently you hone your skills, the stronger your transformation will be, moving you toward being a non-smoker for life.

Going Forward

Once you have reached this point in the process you can completely enjoy your life smoke-free. However, there is one more step necessary to solidify change.

Remaining smoke-free happens on two levels. The first is on the personal level. You have all of the skills, tools, and resources you need to continue living a healthy and happy life. You alone are responsible for your responses and behaviors. It is you alone who ultimately makes the decisions as to what to do and what not to do. Understanding that you have control over your emotions and thoughts means that *you can enjoy greater freedom in who you are as a person.*

Your personal commitment to yourself is by far the most important part of this process. From day one I've asked you to commit to yourself to creating the life you want and deserve. Quitting smoking isn't about making others happy; it's about doing what's best for you. It has to start and end with you.

When you began this book you signed a personal commitment, a promise that you would achieve this goal. It is just as important to keep promises to yourself as it is to keep promises to others. So each and every time you need a reminder, go back and reread the commitment that you made.

Keep in mind we are social creatures. Relationships are a part of the human experience. You have many people in your life who knew you as a smoker and who now have the opportunity to relate to you as a non-smoker. There are also those people you used to smoke with in the past. Many of my clients were unnecessarily worried that they would lose these relationships once they stopped smoking. The truth is that your friends want to be with you because of your personality, not because of that old smoking habit. Similarly, some people incorrectly think that once they become a non-smoker they will have to cut smokers out of their lives. This idea is unhealthy in addition to being untrue. It is important to establish boundaries in terms of your own behavior versus the behavior of others. Even as a non-smoker, you can still spend time with smokers. The big difference now, however, is that you now can choose not to smoke.

I tell clients who are not committed to quitting that I am not the smoking police. It is not my job to make someone else stop smoking. I can certainly help facilitate change for someone who wants to stop smoking, but I don't walk through my day-to-day life forcing change on people. Similarly if you have relationships with people who are still smoking, you will be wise to realize that they have the right to make this choice, and that preaching to them about their need to quit will do no-one any good. If they want to discuss quitting, fantastic; feel free to share with them how you QUIT. If not, that's fine, too; let them be. I mention this because some people experience such a powerful and positive change that they feel the desire to share it with everyone and to get a bit pushy about it. When people are ready to quit, they will. We can still be friends with them and respect them without forcing our point of view on them. If smoking is not a problem for them, then it is not a problem for me, and it shouldn't be for you, either.

The take-home message here is that your relationships are far more important than someone else's habits. Some people think that you should completely avoid people and places that remind you of smoking. I disagree. I subscribe to the school of thought in which the goal of the process is to give you the greatest degree of freedom. Although you may not want to be around friends when they are actually smoking you can still separate people from behavior, and continue to enjoy your relationships.

Since you are a part of a social system, it is important to utilize this system in keeping this change. Just as you have used your own inner skill sets to change you can leverage your relationships to help solidify the change throughout your life. At the start of this process you committed to yourself and now it is time to make the commitment to others.

The final step in staying smoke-free is to let others know that you have QUIT. You have done it for you, and it is important to you. So for the last step, let other people know that you have quit smoking, and how good you feel because of it, and how you did it. You can do this face-to-face, or in writing. So choose at least five people who are the closest to you and tell them face-to-face, or in a letter or an email, that you have committed yourself to being smoke-free forever.

Making this level of social commitment will support you as time goes by. Social commitment has a very strong influence on the unconscious mind. The other component to this is taking pride in what you have achieved. Why not? You have accomplished something that you have set your mind to, perhaps something that you have unsuccessfully tried to do a number of times in the past. This time you are successful, so share that success with those most important to you.

And please accept our sincere congratulations on sticking with us on the journey, on committing to this new behavior, and on successfully becoming a non-smoker for life!

About the Authors

Jess Marion

Hypnosis has been a life long passion for me. Ever since I was young I had a deep curiosity for how the mind works. I can still remember the first time I saw a hypnotist on T.V. who helped someone change their life, I was both amazed and hooked! Since then I have been on an incredible journey.

In 2010 I opened Philadelphia Hypnosis where I still see clients during the week. In 2012 I partnered with Sarah and Shawn Carson and am now a trainer with NLP Training New York. In addition to the NLP, hypnosis, and advanced coaching workshops we also provide private coaching and hypnotherapy services.

Over the years I have worked with hundreds of smoker who have successfully quit. One of the greatest joys in my hypnosis practice is when a new non-smoker throws out those old cigarettes.

I am also the co-author of "Quit: The Hypnotist's Handbook To Running Effective Stop Smoking Sessions", "The Power of Hypnotic Influence", "The Swish", "The Visual Squash", and "Deep Trance Identification: Unconscious Modeling and Mastery for Hypnosis Practitioners, Coaches, and Everyday People"

To discover more visit us at www.bestnlpnewyork.com and www.stop-smoking-nyc.com

Sarah Carson

I am a Certified (H)NLP Trainer, Certified Conversational Hypnosis Trainer, Consulting Hypnotist and Co-Founder and Director of The International Center for Positive Change and Hypnosis.

For many years I have been passionate about understanding how the mind works and my journey has taken my primarily into the world of NLP and Hypnosis. These two areas of study continue to fascinate me and I am always eager to learn more and to share what I learn. During my own personal journey I discovered just how powerful the mind is and more I learned the more I wanted to know. Along the way I also experienced my own personal transformations. These experiences convinced me that NLP and Hypnosis truly work for positive change.

I became an NLP Trainer and Conversational Hypnosis trainer with the express goal of share my understandings and learnings with as many people as possible, to help them change their own lives and transform the lives of others.

At NLP Training New York I teach NLP and hypnosis training courses and also hold private consultations for individual personal transformation.

For me, this is not just a job, it is a passion, a way of life and I am dedicated to helping others learn the skills to transform their lives and live their dreams

I am the co-author of "Quit" and "The Meta Pattern: The Ultimate Structure of Influence"

To discover more visit us at www.bestnlpnewyork.com and www.stop-smoking-nyc.com

Shawn Carson

I was born in Lacashire, England, I moved to New York City in 1996 Since then, as an 'Englishman in New York', I have lived, loved, worked and taught in Manhattan.

Since childhood, I have been fascinated with the Mind. I began to study the application of NLP to sales and management in 1994. Since that time, my interest has grown and I have become a Master Practitioner and Trainer in NLP and Hypnosis Trainer, as well as seeing private clients. In addition I am a Clean Language Facilitator, Reiki Master and practitioner of EFT.

I began to teach NLP and Hypnosis in 2006 and opened the doors of our training and coaching business, IPH (now NLP Training New York), in 2007.

Teaching and helping others in NLP and Hypnosis helps me to understand myself better. After all, at heart we all share the same fears, hopes, dreams.

I am the co-author of six books including "Quit", "The Swish", "The Visual Squash", "Keeping the Brain in Mind", "Deep Trance Identification", and "The Meta Pattern"

To discover more visit us at www.bestnlpnewyork.com and www.stop-smoking-nyc.com

Other Books From This Publisher

Quit: The Hypnotists Handbook to Running Effective Stop Smoking Sessions
By Jess Marion, Sarah Carson and Shawn Carson
Foreword by Igor Ledochowski

NLP Mastery Series: The Swish
By Shawn Carson and Jess Marion
Foreword by John Overdurf

NLP Mastery Series: The Visual Squash
By Jess Marion and Shawn Carson
Foreword by Melissa Tiers

NLP Mastery Series: The Meta Pattern
By Sarah Carson and Shawn Carson
Forward by John Overdurf

Keeping The Brain in Mind: Practical Neuroscience for Coaches, Therapists and Hypnosis Practitioners
By Shawn Carson and Melissa Tiers
Foreword by Lincoln C. Bickford MD, PhD

Deep Trance Identification: Unconscious Modeling and Mastery for Hypnosis Practitioners, Coaches, and Everyday People
By Shawn Carson, Jess Marion, with John Overdurf
Forward by Michael Watson

Made in the USA
Middletown, DE
03 May 2019